WESTERN EUROPE:

WHAT PATH TO INTEGRATION?

PROBLEMS IN POLITICAL SCIENCE
under the editorial direction of NEAL RIEMER, *University of Wisconsin-Milwaukee*

WESTERN EUROPE: WHAT PATH TO INTEGRATION?
edited by CAROL EDLER BAUMANN, *University of Wisconsin-Milwaukee*

THE REPRESENTATIVE: TRUSTEE? DELEGATE? PARTISAN? POLITICO?
edited by NEAL RIEMER, *University of Wisconsin-Milwaukee*

FREE SPEECH AND POLITICAL PROTEST
edited by MARVIN SUMMERS, *University of Wisconsin-Milwaukee*

OTHER VOLUMES IN PREPARATION

PROBLEMS IN POLITICAL SCIENCE

Western Europe:

WHAT PATH TO INTEGRATION?

EDITED WITH AN INTRODUCTION BY
Carol Edler Baumann
University of Wisconsin-Milwaukee

D. C. HEATH AND COMPANY BOSTON

Library of Congress Catalog Card Number: 67-27817

COPYRIGHT © 1967 BY D. C. HEATH AND COMPANY

No part of the material covered by this copyright
may be reproduced in any form without written
permission of the publisher. Printed in the
United States of America

Printed July 1967

Table of Contents

Glossary

Atlantic Alliance—collective defense arrangement between United States and Western Europe; embodied in North Atlantic Treaty of 1949.

Benelux—Belgium, the Netherlands, and Luxembourg formed first post-war European customs union in 1948; joined in Treaty of Economic Union in 1958.

Brussels Treaty—1948 Treaty of Economic, Social, and Cultural Collaboration and Collective Self-Defense; post-war West European collective defense arrangement which became predecessor to NATO.

COMECON—Council for Mutual Economic Assistance (also known as CEMA); East European organization for economic cooperation.

Common Market—popular term for European Economic Community; economic organization aimed at elimination of internal tariffs, creation of common external tariff, and free flow of goods, labor, capital and services among member states.

Council of Europe—created in 1949 to achieve greater unity among members and to realize and preserve common ideals; sounding board for European opinion.

Customs Union—economic organization in which all tariffs and other trade restrictions are eliminated among members and common tariff is applied to all imports from non-member states.

ECA—Economic Cooperation Administration; U. S. Government agency established in 1948 to administer Marshall Plan.

ECSC—European Coal and Steel Community (also known as Schuman Plan); established 1952 to create common market in coal and steel products among member states.

EDC—European Defense Community; abortive proposal to create integrated European Army under control of European Defense Minister and European Assembly; failed ratification by all prospective members.

EEC—European Economic Community (also known as Common Market); economic organization aimed at elimination of internal tariffs, creation of common external tariff, and free flow of goods, labor, capital and services among member states.

EFTA—European Free Trade Association; free trade area of "outer seven" with internal trade barriers eliminated, but no common external tariff toward non-members.

EPC—European Political Community designed as supranational political union based on federal principles and elected representative assembly; never ratified by proposed members.

Euratom—Europlan Atomic Energy Community created in 1958; European body responsible for nuclear research in peaceful uses of atomic energy and for creation of common market in nuclear products.

Free Trade Area—economic organization which aims at elimination of trade barriers between member states but no common external tariff toward non-members; basis of EFTA.

GATT—General Agreement on Tariffs and Trade of 1947; provides rules and machinery for reduction of trade barriers on multilateral, world-wide, and nondiscriminatory basis.

Inner Six—members of ECSC and EEC; Belgium, France, Germany, Italy, Luxembourg, and the Netherlands.

Marshall Plan—developed from 1947 proposal by U.S. Secretary of State George Marshall for European cooperation and U.S. assistance as basis for European economic recovery; led to creation of OEEC.

NATO—North Atlantic Treaty Organization; West European and North American collective defense organization with integrated forces and joint strategic planning which developed out of North Atlantic Treaty of 1949.

North Atlantic Council—body which gives political direction to NATO; consists of Foreign Ministers of member states.

OEEC—Organization for European Economic Cooperation; established in 1947 to determine and coordinate West European recovery needs and to distribute U.S. economic assistance on a regional basis; succeeded by OECD.

OECD—Organization for Economic Cooperation and Development; created in 1961 as transatlantic successor to OEEC for continued economic cooperation among members and coordinated approach to developing states.

Outer Seven—members of EFTA; Austria, Denmark, Norway, Portugal, Sweden, Switzerland, United Kingdom.

SACEUR—Supreme Allied Commander, Europe; military commander of integrated NATO forces in Europe.

Schuman Plan—French proposal to pool coal and steel production and to create a common market for coal and steel products; evolved into ECSC.

SHAPE—Supreme Headquarters, Allied Powers Europe; central headquarters for planning and analysis of NATO strategy.

Treaties of Rome—treaties (signed 1957) establishing the European Economic Community and the European Atomic Energy Community of the "inner six."

Warsaw Pact—Treaty of Friendship, Cooperation, and Mutual Assistance signed at Warsaw in 1955 between Soviet Union and East European states; East European counterpart to NATO.

WEU—Western European Union; with failure of EDC, WEU was created in 1955 as successor to Brussels Treaty and as European component of NATO; members include inner six, plus Britain.

The Clash of Ideas

THE PROGRESS OF INTEGRATION

INTEGRATION IS OVERRATED

[T]he speed and power of the effects of the formative events of 1945–1950, as well as of the effects of the European institutions put into operation thus far, though impressive, may still have been somewhat overrated; . . .

—KARL W. DEUTSCH

INTEGRATION IS REAL AND PERMANENT

Few people believe that the existing system of regional government . . . has a claim to longevity. I believe that it does. Because it corresponds to the nature of the New Europe, . . . it may well be a real system of government rather than a mere temporary style.

—ERNST B. HAAS

NATIONALISM VERSUS SUPRANATIONALISM

A EUROPE OF STATES

[W]hat are the realities of Europe? What are the pillars on which it can be built? The States . . . are the only entities that have the right to order and the authority to act. To imagine that something can be built that would be effective for action and that would be approved by the peoples outside and above the States—this is a dream. . . . at the present time there cannot be any other Europe than a Europe of States. . . .

—CHARLES DE GAULLE

A SUPRANATIONAL EUROPE

No society can function effectively without the exercise of authority. Without such authority European integration cannot be brought about. No measure of integration achieved can be safeguarded without it. . . . The joint exercise of sovereignty which European integration implies must . . . rest with organs possessing the power to discharge their task.

—HANS NORD

THE ATLANTIC FRAMEWORK

ATLANTIC UNION

[A] real Atlantic Community would have to be based on: (1) an
Atlantic common market, and (2) a basic minimum of common
political institutions. . . . the establishment of a political community, however limited its conception, would mean the transfer of
some sovereign rights to a common political authority having *limited
but real* powers.

—MAURICE ALLAIS

ATLANTIC PARTNERSHIP

. . . Atlantic Union never became a matter of serious inter-governmental negotiation. Today . . . it is hard to discern either popular or
governmental support for this approach—especially in Europe. . . .
The [other] policy choice is the concept of partnership with a uniting
Europe. 'Partnership' is a confining word. But . . . it conveys a
sweeping concept—the idea of a united Europe with which the
United States could work in close cooperation and on equal terms.

—J. ROBERT SCHAETZEL

Introduction

In the past quarter century the states of Western Europe have not only survived the destruction and despair scattered in the wake of World War II, but have emerged from that havoc both economically revitalized and politically self-confident. Disillusioned with the suicidal futility of intra-European strife and fearful of a new wave of expansion from the East, Western Europe united to a degree unprecedented in modern times. Interwoven through the foreign policy motifs of the period and underlying their basic assumptions and objectives, the theme of integration—political, military, and economic—has permeated the substance of postwar European politics. That theme is the subject of this volume.

In any examination of current international phenomena, the student is inclined to pose such relevant and pragmatic questions as: "Why did it happen?"; "What are the problems?"; and "Where do we go from here?" Through selected readings, therefore, this volume will attempt to illustrate: (1) both the positive and negative motivations behind the movement for closer European union; (2) the continuing and all-pervasive issues which have appeared throughout the unification process; and (3) the possible alternative paths that integration might take in the future. Both the analytical framework of the book and the thrust of its selections focus upon rationale, problems, and alternatives, not upon historical background, chronological developments, or institutional structures.

I

From what sources did the movement for European integration receive its impetus? What were the reasons which motivated European leaders to make the policy decisions and to take the policy actions necessary to raise the concept of unification from the books of philosophers to the agenda of governments? After all, the idea of European union was not a new one. The proposal for a permanent European government emerged as early as the Conciliar Movement of the 15th Century and the concept of European unification as a means to "perpetual peace" received the periodic attention of numerous writers (if not that of statesmen) up to the present. The 20th

Century witnessed further progress when the League of Nations officially discussed the Briand Memorandum's suggestion for European political union. Yet no action was taken. What, then, is that unique combination of circumstance, thought, and action which has made possible the more recent advances toward closer integration? A few possible answers are suggested in some of the major speeches of the period by those in—and out—of office.

Both negative and positive rationale are clearly evident in the early postwar appeals for closer cooperation or union between the states of Western Europe. A revulsion against the carnage of the war created widespread disillusionment with the unbridled nationalism which many felt had been a major cause of the war itself. To avoid a repetition of such fratricide, it was argued, the European nation-states should submerge, or at least modify, their separate sovereignties and unite within the larger entity of "Europe." Thus aware of the frailties of nationalism, even that wartime symbol of the English nation, Winston Churchill, could argue that the only remedy for the states of Europe was ". . . to recreate the European family . . . and to provide it with a structure under which it can dwell in peace, in safety and in freedom. We must build," he said, "a kind of United States of Europe."

Just as significant as the realization that the European states divided against each other could not survive, was the fear that a divided Europe could not withstand the onslaught of a common external enemy. Though anxieties about a resurgent Germany had not disappeared by the late 1940's, they had been joined by the equally disquieting fears of a militarily strong and potentially dangerous Communist Russia. Soviet expansion in Eastern Europe lent credence to the image of a "common enemy" which provided the theme of British Foreign Minister Bevin's famous "Western Union" speech of January, 1948. In it he outlined in blunt terms the Soviet policies of "cutting off Eastern Europe from the rest of the world and turning it into an exclusively self-contained bloc under the control of Moscow and Communist party." He then maintained that all these developments ". . . point to the conclusion that the free nations of Western Europe must now draw closely together." It was the negative force of fear, then, which led to the creation of the collective defense Brussels Treaty Organization and, ultimately, to NATO.

In similar fashion, the concrete imperatives of economic survival—first, economic recovery from the devastation of the war and, second, a concern for future development in both the industrial and agricultural sectors—spurred the drive for economic cooperation and bore fruit in the Marshall Plan and the Organization for European Economic Cooperation. The selection by then Secretary of State George Marshall is included less for its detailed proposals (of which there were few), than for its underlying theme of self help, mutual aid, and European cooperation as the continuing principles which should guide Europe back onto the path toward recovery and development. The United States would provide assistance for that process, Marshall said, but "The initiative . . . must come from Europe. . . . The program should be a joint one, agreed to by a number, if not all European nations." With a positive European response to the Marshall offer, Western Europe embarked upon the first steps toward a more logical rationalization of its economy through increased production, freer trade, and convertibility of currencies; it thereby established a firm foundation for the successful construction of such subsequent structures as the Coal and Steel Community and the Common Market.

Along with those who deplored the tragedy of aggressive nationalism and those who recognized the need for military unity and economic cooperation, were those who attacked the European state system *per se*. With an argument somewhat broader in its implications, the proponents of this position maintained that the entire rationale for the nation-state as the basic unit of world organization was no longer valid—especially in Europe—and that modern production and trade, to say nothing of military technology, made European integration the logical, if not necessary, path of the future. Politically as well, they argued, Europe could only reassert itself as a leading actor in world affairs if it shed the divisive patterns of past rivalries and united as a single state or confederation.

These "pro-Europeans" were divided in early years both in goals and in approaches. First, there were those who favored the creation of a tightly integrated federal Europe (the federalists) and those who preferred the development of a looser configuration or confederal structure (the confederalists or non-federalists). There was also a marked division between the constitutionalist approach (the drafting of conventions or constitutions for a political union under a European parliament or government) and the functionalist approach (uniting for specific purposes or functions and advancing toward political unity by practical cooperation, generally in economic matters).

Although the goal battle is still being fought, the functional method clearly emerged as the dominant theme of European integration when the functionalists survived as the successful exponents of such vital experiments in integration as the Schuman Plan and the Common Market. Jean Monnet, father of the Schuman Plan and one of the principal spokesmen for the functional approach to integration, thus emphasized in positive fashion the opportunities for a united Europe in his speech on the value of common institutions. In a subsequent article, J.B. Duroselle maintains that it was exactly this emphasis upon what Monnet calls "the extraordinary transforming power of common institutions" which provided his unique contribution to the theory and practice of European integration.

II

The selections in Section II focus on the continuing problems of integration which have appeared in all areas—political, military, and economic—and which have persisted in one form or another throughout the integration process. One of the most pervasive of these problems has been nationalism itself and its continuing influence on the national policies of the states of Western Europe. Thus, nationalism versus supranationalism became a prime issue in the British parliamentary and press debates of the 1950's regarding membership in the European Coal and Steel Community and later in the proposed European Defense Community. In the 1960's it emerged once again as a major factor in President de Gaulle's thinking about the future form of the Common Market and the powers of its "supranational" Commission. Should, or can, the historical contributions and the psychological gratifications of nationalism be submerged to promote the novel experiment called supranationalism? Should, or can, the *states* of Europe become "Europe"? These are the questions, both in their normative and in their more empirical form, which not only plagued the statesmen of Europe, but which must be considered by any serious student of European integration today.

The specific issues concerning Britain's relationship to the continent do not lend themselves easily to a pro or con analysis. The nub of the dilemma which faced the United Kingdom could be posed only superficially as a question of "to join or not to join"; more accurately it should be regarded as a matter of "how far?" and "in what way?" The Baumann and Camps articles, therefore, illustrate the changing nature of British policies toward the continent as they developed from an early emphasis upon close association to the 1961 decision to apply for full membership in the European Economic Community. The first selection points to the free trade area negotiations of 1958–1959 as providing significant insights into the "agonizing reappraisal" of the British position at that time. Inextricably linked within and yet torn between the three worlds of the Commonwealth, the United States, and Western Europe, Britain was alternately attracted by the advantages and repulsed by the disadvantages of participation in European Union. The Camps excerpt outlines the major factors which led to the shift in British attitudes; she concludes that ". . . the controlling consideration was the belief that Britain would have more influence—in Europe, with the United States and in the world generally—as a member of the European Community than it would alone." Together, both articles provide a relevant framework for understanding the continuing British dilemma regarding the Common Market, the impact of the French veto upon it, and the significance of the British Labour Government's recent decision to submit a second application for membership—and de Gaulle's reaction to it.

Equal in complexity to the relationship between Britain and the continent and central to the future of Western Europe as a whole, "the German problem" has hovered with perplexing persistence over the scene of European unification. As Germany's role within Europe evolved from defeated enemy to responsible member of the European family, the character of that problem also changed. The early Adenauer decision to integrate West Germany tightly into the developing institutional structure of Western Europe has been closely adhered to by his successors, and up to the present time it has not met with any serious challenge within the Federal Republic. Views have differed, however, regarding the nature of that structure and, more importantly, its temporary or permanent status. Should the Federal Republic continue to cast its lot within the framework of a united Western Europe or should it seek German reunification within a larger entity including both Western and Eastern Europe? Can such an entity be created without destroying the integration already achieved within the West? These are the questions to which the selections by Knappstein and Hartmann address themselves.

But the German problem can be understood fully only within the broader context of a divided Europe—East and West. Selections nine and ten are devoted to that topic. In his article on Communist views of European integration, Marshall Shulman examines the impact of the successes of the Common Market both on Communist ideology and on Marxist analyses of Western economic developments. He then proceeds to delineate the effects of such analyses on Soviet strategic thinking and policies toward the West. Zbigniew Brzezinski, in turn, examines the practical impact which the Common Market has had upon the Soviet Union's European economic policies. He particularly points up the attraction which West European integration has exerted upon the East Europeans and argues that "American collaboration with Europe to reunite Europe and to reintegrate Russia into the Western civilization [*is*] in harmony with both American and European long-range interests. . . . Step by step," he concludes, "the East European states should be encouraged to become associated, remotely and indirectly at first, and then more and more closely and directly, with the Common Market." The divisive forces of the Cold War, thus reflected in the politico-ideological division of Europe between East and West, are viewed in both articles as having so influenced the integration process as to create the unstable unification of what can be at most only a truncated continent.

The final selections in Section II consider the unique set of ties between Western Europe and the United States—what they have been, what they are, and what they should be. Outlining the basic interests and values which the Atlantic states possess in common, Robert Bowie, a former Assistant Secretary of State for Policy Planning, presents in lucid style the argument that an integrated Europe in an Atlantic partnership is the best answer to the question of how the West should organize itself. Though firmly maintaining that an integrated European community and an Atlantic partnership complement each other, Mr. Bowie proceeds with a closer examination of the strains currently existing within the Atlantic relationship and hence endangering it. He points to the European desire for a greater role in world affairs as both understandable and valid, yet incapable of complete fulfillment. The crux of the problem, as Bowie regards it, is that ". . . the Europe which would be a full partner is only emergent, yet the Europeans want and expect to be treated as equal partners already."

Viewed in the context of such an analysis, General de Gaulle's challenge both to the concept of an integrated European community and to an Atlantic partnership becomes even more serious than it might otherwise appear. Much of the strength of that challenge is derived from the tensions already present in the "unequal partnership" which he assails both as impinging on national sovereignty and as inconsistent with an independent European policy. Thus, even when Washington has abandoned its obsession with de Gaulle as the *bête noire* of further European integration, the issues which he has raised will remain. And regardless of the path to integration which Western Europe may ultimately embark upon, its relations with the United States will be of prime importance for the progress of its journey.

III

In the concluding section of the volume the selections illustrate alternative patterns of integration. Although current organizations may be categorized as to their predominantly political, military, or economic orientation, the debate surrounding future steps toward integration has not centered on any particular one of these approaches. Rather, it has concerned itself (1) with the processes and progress of integration to date—whether supranational integration has in fact "succeeded" in Europe or has already reached its high water mark and will now recede, (2) with the degree of cohesion most desirable —whether Europe should develop as a Europe of states or as an integrated community, and (3) with the kind of Atlantic framework within which a united Europe can best exist—whether it should be closely integrated within an Atlantic Community or become an equal partner in a looser Atlantic partnership. The related question of whether or not Western Europe should attempt to operate independently of the Atlantic Alliance—perhaps as a third force—or remain within that framework, whatever its ultimate political form, is discussed in the section dealing with Western Europe and the United States.

The Deutsch, Haas, and Aron articles attempt to assess the progress of the integration movement and the processes by which it has developed since the late 1940's. Karl Deutsch examines existing European organizations with regard to their membership, their functions, and their allocation of roles, expectations, and rewards. Deutsch is sceptical of the "spill-over" theory whereby the proponents of further integration have argued that each step of functional integration in one area will lead to other steps in other areas and so accelerate the whole process. He argues that in the 1950's "spill-over" was less effective in practice than suggested in theory and concludes that the immediate future, at least, may still belong to the sovereign state. Ernst Haas, in contrast, defends the thesis that experience not only has confirmed the validity of the "spill-over" theory but has implied the future continuation of the "spill-over" process. Haas argues, in fact, that because it corresponds to the true nature of the

New Europe, supranational integration has made its claim to longevity and future progress.

Raymond Aron, the French political sociologist, appears less optimistic of the possibilities, or, more to the point, more sceptical of the rationale for supranationalism in his article, "Old Nations, New Europe." After admitting that the West European states "have learned to live together and to live in peace," that economic cooperation has become the rule, and that Britain's exclusion from the E.E.C. should not be magnified into catastrophic proportions, Aron nonetheless concludes with this pertinent observation:

"The old nations still live in the hearts of men, and love of the European nation is not yet born—assuming that it ever will be. But the federation of the Old Continent is held in check less by the survival of nationalism, large or small, than by another cause, simpler and often unrecognized: the present mixture of cooperation and integration in Europe and within the Atlantic Alliance is sufficient to assure the achievement of prosperity and security. It is not sufficient to create a European state. Rather, one must ask: What would be the object of a European state? To have a sense of vocation, Europe would have to discover a goal."

In addition to the different scholarly assessments which exist regarding the processes of integration and their successes or failures in attainment, there are equally divergent views concerning what degree of integration is in fact desirable and what patterns should be followed for the future. Are the real sources of power and policy in Europe, as de Gaulle insists, basically the states themselves? If so, is he correct in concluding that "there cannot be any other Europe than a Europe of States"? Or, can a supranational Europe with common institutions be created as the new Europe? Should it be? Jean Monnet, early spokesman of the European movement, has consistently maintained that it can—and should. Moreover, he has argued that a "Europe of Nations" without such common institutions would be not only inadequate, but dangerous.

Hans Nord, in his defense of supranationalism, argues that the joint exercise of political authority is essential to the successful implementation of European integration and that such authority, in turn, must rest with European organs possessing the necessary power to carry out their functions. Essentially, within the concept of supranationalism, he proposes a federal structure with a division of powers between Europe as a whole and the separate nations composing Europe. However, he argues, this European Community must not operate entirely through member *governments,* but rest directly upon the *peoples* of Europe; it thus requires a European parliament, directly elected. Despite his argument, Nord does not fail to recognize the presence and value of diversity in Europe when he quotes the Luxembourg maxim, "Wir wollen bleiben was wir sind,"—we will remain what we are!

Opposed to both Monnet and Nord, Charles de Gaulle stands forth as the new champion of nationalism and the state system. De Gaulle, as he tells us in his *War Memoirs,* has always thought of his own country "as dedicated to an exalted and exceptional destiny. . . . France cannot be France without greatness." Thus, a great Frenchman, General de Gaulle has regarded France and the other states of Europe as the only possible pillars upon which a united Europe can be built. Or, in his own words, "The States are, in truth, certainly very different from one another, each of which has its own spirit, its own history, its own language, its own misfortunes, glories and ambitions; but these States are the only entities that have the right to order and the authority to act. To imagine that something can be built that would be effective for action and that would be approved by the peoples outside and above the States—this is a dream." This view of the state and others which also reflect de Gaulle's concept of Europe are effectively contrasted with Jean Monnet's Europe in the selection by J.B. Duroselle who concludes that the two concepts are so contradictory that no compromise, but only a choice between them, is possible.

The last two selections in the volume advocate two different ways of organizing European relationships within a larger Atlantic framework. Although it can be persuasively argued, as J. Robert Schaetzel has done, that there are three broad alternatives for the organization of West European and North American relations, the first—a continuation of the traditional nation-state system—has already been discussed *inter alia* in the selections dealing with nationalism and supranationalism and within the speeches of General de Gaulle. The two remaining alternatives of an integrated "Atlantic Community" or an "Atlantic Partnership" of equals are presented most effectively in the articles by Allais and Schaetzel. Maurice Allais advocates the creation of a federal Atlantic Union or Community in his article on "An Integrated Atlantic Community." As with the proponents of a federated European Community, M. Allais proposes at the least the creation of an Atlantic common market and a basic minimum of common political institutions. The third alternative of an "Atlantic

Partnership" is analyzed and advocated by J. Robert Schaetzel, American Ambassador to the European Communities. Emphasizing the realities of trans-Atlantic interdependence, he concludes that the old patterns are simply inadequate and that the creation of new relationships which reflect those realities are therefore imperative.

The continuing issues of West European integration provide both provocative and informative subject matter for the student of international relations and international organization. They are also significant for the content and conduct of American foreign relations as they relate to present and future policies toward Europe—East and West. It can even be argued convincingly that the processes and problems of integration in Western Europe provide invaluable lessons for the embryonic unification experiments currently taking place in Latin America and Africa. This volume is thus designed not only to acquaint the student with those problems, but to provide him with different and sometimes conflicting views concerning their solution so that he may be better equipped to understand them and their relevance to the general study of political science and international relations.

I Rationale for Unification: Dangers and Opportunities

THE TRAGEDY OF EUROPEAN NATIONALISM

WINSTON CHURCHILL

Let Europe Arise!

Sir Winston Churchill (1874–1965), renowned world states-
man, British politician, and versatile historian, began his
political career in 1899 when he entered British politics as a
Conservative; he won his first seat in the House of Com-
mons the following year. After an interlude with the Liberal
Party, Churchill returned to Conservatism and led the war-
time coalition government as Prime Minister from 1940
until 1945. As opposition leader in the post-war period, he
headed the United Europe Movement in Britain and emerged,
along with Coudenhove-Kalergi, Spaak, Reynaud, and
Monnet, as an influential advocate of European Union.
During this period, Churchill delivered numerous speeches
both in Britain and on the continent in favor of closer
European unification; of these, his address on September 19,
1946, at the University of Zurich, reprinted below, was one
of the most widely publicized.
*   Though he had never specified what the exact relationship*
of the United Kingdom to the continent should be, when he
returned to office in 1951 the pro-Europeans were disillu-

From Winston Churchill, *Vital Speeches of the Day.* Vol. 12, No. 24 (October 1, 1946). It may
also be found in *The Sinews of Peace* "Post-War Speeches by Winston S. Churchill," ed.
Randolph S. Churchill (London: Cassell & Company, Ltd., 1948), pp. 198–202.

sioned by his unwillingness to accept British membership in such supranational organizations as the European Coal and Steel Community and the proposed European Defense Community. Nonetheless, as Prime Minister, Churchill led the drive for the creation of the Western European Union defense organization, when the European Defense Community failed in 1954. Retaining his seat in Parliament, Churchill resigned as Prime Minister in April, 1955.

I WISH TO SPEAK TO YOU today about the tragedy of Europe. This noble continent, comprising on the whole the fairest and the most cultivated regions of the earth, enjoying a temperate and equable climate, is the home of all the great parent races of the Western world. It is the foundation of Christian faith and Christian ethics.

It is the origin of most of the culture, art, philosophy and science, both of ancient and modern times. If Europe were once united in the sharing of its common inheritance there would be no limit to the happiness, the prosperity and the glory which its 300,000,000 or 400,000,000 people would enjoy. Yet it is from Europe that has sprung that series of frightful and nationalistic morals originated by the Teutonic nations in their rise to power, which we have seen in this twentieth century and which have for a long time wrecked the peace and marred the prospects of all mankind.

And what is the plight to which Europe has been reduced? Some of the smaller states have indeed made a good recovery, but over wide areas a vast quivering mass of tormented, hungry, careworn and bewildered human beings gaze on the ruins of their cities and scan the dark horizon for the approach of some new peril, tyranny or terror.

Among the victors there is a babel of voices, among the vanquished a sullen silence of despair.

That is all that Europeans, grouped in so many ancient states and nations—that is all that the Germanic races have got by tearing each other to pieces and spreading havoc far and wide. Indeed, but for the fact that the great republic across the Atlantic Ocean has at length realized that the ruin or enslavement of Europe has involved their own fate as well, and has stretched out hands of succor and guidance—but for that, the Dark Ages would have returned in all their cruelty and squalor.

They may still return. There is a remedy which, if it were generally and spontaneously adopted by the great majority of people in the many lands, would, as if by a miracle, transform the whole scene and would in a few years make all Europe, or the greater part of it, as free and as happy as Switzerland is today.

What is this sovereign remedy?

It is to recreate the European family, or as much of it as we can, and to provide it with a structure under which it can dwell in peace, in safety and in freedom. We must build a kind of United States of Europe. In this way only will hundreds of millions of toilers be able to regain the simple joys and hopes which make life worth living.

The process is simple. All that is needed is the resolve of hundreds of millions of men and women to do right instead of wrong and to gain as their reward blessing instead of cursing. Much work has been done upon this task by the exertions of the planned European Union, which owes so much to Count Coudenhove-Kalergi and which demanded the services of the famous French patron and statesman, Aristide Briand.

There is also that immense body of doctrine and procedure which was brought into being amid high hopes after the first World War. I mean the League of Nations. The League of Nations did not fail because of its principles or conceptions. It failed because these principles were deserted by those states who had brought it into being. It failed because the Governments of those days feared to face the facts and act while time remained.

This disaster must not be repeated. There is, therefore, much knowledge and material with which to build and also bitter, dear-bought experience to spur the builders.

. . . [W]hy should there not be a European grouping which can give a sense of national patriotism and common citizenship to the distracted peoples of this turbulent and mighty Continent, and why should it not take its proper, rightful place, with other great groupings and help to shape the destinies of man?

In order that this may be accomplished, there must be an act of faith in which millions of families speaking many languages must consciously take part. We all know that the two world wars through which we have passed arose out of a vain passion of a newly united Germany to play a dominating part in the world. In this last struggle crimes and massacres have been committed which have no parallel since the invasion of the Mongols in the fourteenth century and have no equal at any time in human history.

The guilty must be punished. Germany must be deprived of the power to rearm and make another aggressive war. But when all this has been done, as it will be done, as it is being done, then there must be an end to retribution.

There must be what Mr. Gladstone called a blessed act of oblivion. We must all turn our backs upon the horrors of the past. We must look to the future. We cannot afford to drag forward across the years that are to come the hatreds and revenges which have sprung from the injuries of the past.

If Europe is to be saved from infinite misery and, indeed, from final doom, there must be this act of faith in the European family and this act of oblivion against all the crimes and follies of the past, and the free peoples of Europe must rise to the height of these resolves of the soul and of the instinct of the spirit of man.

If they can, the wrongs and injuries which have been inflicted will have been washed away on all sides by the miseries which have been endured.

Is there any need for any further conflicts or agony? Is the only lesson of history to be that mankind is unteachable? Let there be justice, mercy and freedom. The people have only to will it in order to achieve their hearts' desire.

I am now going to say something which will astonish you. The first step in the re-creation of the European family must be a partnership between France and Germany.

In this way only can France recover the moral and cultural leadership of Europe.

There can be no revival of Europe without a spiritually great France and a spiritually great Germany.

The structure of the United States of Europe, if well and truly built, will be such as to make the material strength of a single state less important.

Small nations will count as much as large ones and gain their honor by their contribution to the common cause. The ancient states and principalities of Germany, newly joined together into a federal system, might take their individual place among the United States of Europe.

I shall not try to make a detailed program for hundreds of millions of people who want to be happy, free and prosperous, and wish to enjoy the four freedoms of which the great President Roosevelt spoke, and live under the principles embodied in the Atlantic Charter.

If this is the wish of Europeans in so many lands, then they have only to say so and means can certainly be found and machinery erected to carry that wish to full fruition. But I must give warning; time may be short. At present there may be a breathing space. The cannons have ceased firing. The fighting has stopped, but the dangers have not stopped.

If we are to form a United States of Europe, or whatever name it may take, we must begin now. . . .

I must now sum up the propositions which are before us. Our constant aim must be to build and fortify the strength of the United Nations organization. Under and within that world concept, we must recreate the European family in a regional structure, called, it may be, the United States of Europe, and the first practical step would be to form a Council of Europe.

If at first all states of Europe are not willing or able to join the union, we must nevertheless proceed to assemble and combine those who will and can. The salvation of the people, of the common people of every race and land, from war and servitude must be established on solid foundations, and must be guarded by the readiness of all men and women to die rather than to submit to tyranny.

In all this urgent work, France and Germany must take the lead together. Great Britain, the British Commonwealth of Nations, mighty America and, I trust, Soviet Russia—and then indeed all would be well—must be the friends and sponsors of the new Europe. Let Europe arise!

THE DANGERS OF DISUNITY AND ECONOMIC DISARRAY

GEORGE C. MARSHALL

The Need for Economic Cooperation

General George C. Marshall (1880–1959) was Chief of Staff of the U.S. Army during World War II and served as United States Secretary of State from 1947 until 1949 during which period two of the most important early proposals for European cooperation were advanced and adopted—the Organization for European Economic Cooperation and NATO. In his speech at Harvard University on June 5, 1947, Secretary Marshall emphasized the needs of economic recovery and outlined a program of European cooperation and U.S. assistance which later became known as "the Marshall Plan." This plan was implemented in the United States through the European Recovery Program and in Europe by the O.E.E.C. Secretary Marshall also participated in the 1948 negotiations which led to the creation of NATO and, as Secretary of Defense in 1950–51, he assisted in the military implementation of the North Atlantic Treaty.

. . . [T]HE WORLD SITUATION is very serious. . . . I think one difficulty is that the problem is one of such enormous complexity that the very mass of facts presented to the public by press and radio

From George C. Marshall, The Department of State *Bulletin.* Vol. XVI, No. 415 (June 15, 1947), pp. 1159–1160. It may also be found in *Vital Speeches of the Day.* Vol. 13, No. 18 (July 1, 1947).

make it exceedingly difficult for the man in the street to reach a clear appraisement of the situation. Furthermore, the people of this country are distant from the troubled areas of the earth and it is hard for them to comprehend the plight and consequent reactions of the long-suffering peoples, and the effect of those reactions on their governments in connection with our efforts to promote peace in the world.

In considering the requirements for the rehabilitation of Europe the physical loss of life, the visible destruction of cities, factories, mines and railroads was correctly estimated, but it has become obvious during recent months that this visible destruction was probably less serious than the dislocation of the entire fabric of European economy. For the past ten years conditions have been highly abnormal. The feverish preparation for war and the more feverish maintenance of the war effort engulfed all aspects of national economics. Machinery has fallen into disrepair or is entirely obsolete. Under the arbitrary and destructive Nazi rule, virtually every possible enterprise was geared into the German war machine. Long-standing commercial ties, private institutions, banks, insurance companies and shipping companies disappeared, through loss of capital, absorption through nationalization or by simple destruction. In many countries, confidence in the local currency has been severely shaken. The breakdown of the business structure of Europe during the war was complete. Recovery has been seriously retarded by the fact that two years after the close of hostilities a peace settlement with Germany and Austria has not been agreed upon. But even given a more prompt solution of these difficult problems, the rehabilitation of the economic structure of Europe quite evidently will require a much longer time and greater effort than had been foreseen.

There is a phase of this matter which is both interesting and serious. The farmer has always produced the foodstuffs to exchange with the city dweller for the other necessities of life. This division of labor is the basis of modern civilization. At the present time it is threatened with breakdown. The town and city industries are not producing adequate goods to exchange with the food-producing farmer. Raw materials and fuel are in short supply. Machinery is lacking or worn out. The farmer or the peasant cannot find the goods for sale which he desires to purchase. So the sale of his farm produce for money which he cannot use seems to him an unprofitable transaction. He, therefore, has withdrawn many fields from crop cultivation and is using them for grazing. He feeds more grain to stock and finds for himself and his family an ample supply of food, however short he may be on clothing and the other ordinary gadgets of civilization. Meanwhile people in the cities are short of food and fuel. So the governments are forced to use their foreign money and credits to procure these necessities abroad. This process exhausts funds which are urgently needed for reconstruction. Thus a very serious situation is rapidly developing which bodes no good for the world. The modern system of the division of labor upon which the exchange of products is based is in danger of breaking down.

The truth of the matter is that Europe's requirements for the next three or four years of foreign food and other essential products— principally from America—are so much greater than her present ability to pay that she must have substantial additional help, or face economic, social and political deterioration of a very grave character.

The remedy lies in breaking the vicious circle and restoring the confidence of the European people in the economic future of their own countries and of Europe as a whole. The manufacturer and the farmer throughout wide areas must be able and willing to exchange their products for currencies the continuing value of which is not open to question.

Aside from the demoralizing effect on the world at large and the possibilities of disturbances arising as a result of the desperation of the people concerned, the consequences to the economy of the United States should be apparent to all. It is logical that the United States should do whatever it is able to do to assist in the return of normal economic health in the world, without which there can be no political stability and no assured peace. Our policy is directed not against any country or doctrine but against hunger, poverty, desperation and chaos. Its purpose should be the revival of a working economy in the world so as to permit the emergence of political and social conditions in which free institutions can exist. Such assistance, I am convinced, must not be on a piece-meal basis as various crises develop. Any assistance that this Government may render in the future should provide a cure rather than a mere palliative. Any government that is willing to assist in the task of recovery will find full cooperation, I am sure, on the part of the United States Government. Any government which maneuvers to block the recovery of other countries cannot expect help from us. Furthermore, governments, political parties or groups which seek to perpetuate human misery in order to profit therefrom politically or otherwise will encounter the opposition of the United States.

It is already evident that, before the United States Government can proceed much further in its efforts to alleviate the situation and help start the European world on its way to recovery, there must be some agreement among the countries of Europe as to the requirements of the situation and the part those countires themselves will take in order to give proper effect to whatever action might be undertaken by this Government. It would be neither fitting nor efficacious for this Government to undertake to draw up unilaterally a program designed to place Europe on its feet economically. This is the business of the Europeans. The initiative, I think, must come from Europe. The role of this country should consist of friendly aid in the drafting of a European program and of later support of such a program so far as it may be practical for us to do so. The program should be a joint one, agreed to by a number, if not all European nations.

An essential part of any successful action on the part of the United States is an understanding on the part of the people of America of the character of the problem and the remedies to be applied. Political passion and prejudice should have no part. With foresight, and a willingness on the part of our people to face up to the vast responsibility which history has clearly placed upon our country, the difficulties I have outlined can and will be overcome.

ERNEST BEVIN

The Fear of Soviet Expansion

Ernest Bevin (1881–1951) was British Foreign Minister in the postwar Labour government from 1945 until 1951. A trade unionist by background, Bevin became a prominent leader of the British Labour movement and helped establish the Transport and General Workers' Union in 1921. He served in the Churchill coalition government as Minister of Labour and National Service and was subsequently appointed by Prime Minister Attlee as Foreign Secretary. In that position, he seized the initiative presented to Europe in the Marshall speech of 1947 and piloted the negotiations which led to the creation of the O.E.E.C. The following speech, delivered in the British House of Commons on January 22, 1948, along with the Czechoslovakian coup d'etat *of February, 1948, provided the impetus behind the drive for Western Union which in turn led to the creation of NATO in 1949.*

Bevin's early recognition and public pronouncement of the dangers of Soviet expansion, his lead in the creation of Western Union (the Brussels Treaty collective defense organization) in response, and his promotion of the North Atlantic Alliance constituted major contributions to the development and strengthening of Western unity.

WE ARE INDEED at a critical moment in the organization of the post-war world and decisions we now take . . . will be vital to the future peace of the world. What, however, I have first to put before the House is the factual background against which decisions must now be taken. . . .

From Ernest Bevin, *Parliamentary Debates,* House of Commons Official Report, 5th Series (H. M. S. O., London), Vol. 446, Cols. 383–409. It may also be found in *Vital Speeches of the Day.* Vol. 14, No. 8 (February 1, 1948).

The story begins with a series of conferences which were held during the war and at which many ideas were formed. Some were crystallized. Some were not. In this connection, of the political developments that have taken place, one of the main issues at that time affecting the line of subsequent policy which was connected with the future of Poland, the solution arrived at at Yalta, was looked upon by His Majesty's Government at that time as a sensible compromise between conflicting elements, but there is no doubt that as it has evolved it has revealed a policy on the part of the Soviet Union to use every means in their power to get Communist control in Eastern Europe and, as it now appears, in the West as well. It therefore matters little how we temporize and maybe appease, or try to make arrangements. It has been quite clear, I think, that the Communist process goes ruthlessly on in each country. We have seen the game played out in Poland, Bulgaria, Hungary, more recently in Rumania, and from information in our possession other attempts may be made elsewhere. Thus the issue is not simply the organization of Poland or any other country, but the control of Eastern Europe by Soviet Russia whose frontiers have in effect been advanced to Stettin, Trieste and the Elbe. One has only to look at the map to see how, since the war, Soviet Russia has expanded and now stretches from the middle of Europe to the Kurile islands and Sakhalin. Yet all the evidence is that she is not satisfied with this tremendous expansion. In Trieste we have difficulties. We had hoped that the method of international agreement would be allowed to work but it has not been allowed to work, and so what should have been a great experiment in post-war international collaboration has only been a continuing source of friction and bother.

Then we have the great issue in Greece, which is similar to the others I have mentioned. It has been assumed—in fact said—that the Soviet Union can wait; that the United States of America and Great Britain will get tired; and that the so-called government of Communist rebels can be recognized later on without danger; and then in the end that a Communist government will be forced upon Greece and she will be incorporated in the Soviet system of communism with the rest. Here let me make His Majesty's Government's position quite clear. We had hoped to have been out of Greece. We had hoped that after the first election, a government would be formed and in time subsequent elections would take place and the whole process of democratic development would be allowed to function. But that has not been allowed because a state of virtual civil war has been perpetuated the whole time. So it is not a question of what sort of elected government there is in Greece—liberal coalition or whatever it might be—but it is a ruthless attempt constantly maintained to bring that country in the Soviet orbit. . . .

We have had other examples since the war which I need not go into now, wars of nerves and pressure upon weaker neighbors. It is the considered view of His Majesty's Government that attempts to settle international affairs by political barrages and by wars of nerves, reduce the chances of finding acceptable solutions and make agreement difficult, if not impossible. Propaganda is not a contribution to the settlement of international problems. They are all so important that the only way to solve them is coolly and calmly to deal with them on their merits. So much for the brief background of Eastern Europe.

. . . The conception of the unity of Europe and the preservation of Europe as the heart of western civilization is accepted by most people. The importance of this has become increasingly apparent, not only to all the European nations as a result of the post-war crises through which Europe has passed and is passing, but to the whole world. No one disputes the idea of European unity, that is not the issue. The issue is whether European unity cannot be achieved without the domination and control of one great power and that is the issue which has to be solved.

. . . His Majesty's Government cannot agree to four-power cooperation while one of those four powers proceeds to impose its political and economic system on the smaller states. On the contrary, as public opinion in those states changes, and as their economic and social development progresses, none of them will willingly submit to the great powers interfering and preventing the introduction of economic changes, or any other changes, which they deem to be for their own good.

But there is another factor giving great cause for anxiety. It evolved largely with Hitler and Mussolini, and now, I am afraid, it has become an instrument of a very dangerous kind in Europe, and that is what we describe as the Police State. We did not imagine that this would be maintained after the war, but it is and it is carried out with ruthless efficiency. I must say, while we here talk about elections and democracy that where the Police State exists, votes count for very little. It is true that the votes have not disappeared, but it is the voter himself who disappears, and the successful candidate if he dares to have an opinion of his own.

. . . We have always accepted—I would emphasize this and I repeat it now—that the friendliest relations should exist between Russia and the states on the Russian frontier—indeed not only on the frontier—we want these friendly relations with everybody. It is madness to think of anything else if we are ever to have peace.

That is quite a different thing from cutting off Eastern Europe from the rest of the world and turning it into an exclusively self-contained bloc under the control of Moscow and Communist party. The European Recovery Programme brought all this to a head and made us all face up to the problem of the future organization. We did not press the Western Union and I know that some of our neighbors were not desirous of pressing it in the hope that when we got the German-Austrian peace settlements agreement between the Four Powers would close the breach between East and West and thus avoid the necessity of crystallizing Europe into separate blocs. We have always wanted the widest conception of Europe including of course Russia. It is not a new idea. The idea of closer relationship between the countries of Western Europe first arose during the war and in the days of the coalition,—it was discussed already in 1944,—there was talk between my predecessor and the Russian Government about a Western association. His Majesty's Government at that time indicated to the Soviet Government that they would put the establishment of a world organization first on their list. In any case they proposed to rely on the Anglo-Soviet Alliance for the purpose of containing Germany and eventually there might be similar arrangements between France and Great Britain and France and the Soviet Union for this purpose. That was in 1944. We also indicated that it might be desirable to have defense arrangements with Western Europe for the purpose of instituting a common defense policy against the possible revival of German aggression and to determine what role each state should play in the matter of armaments and the disposal of forces. We indicated that when these matters arose we would keep the Soviet Government informed which we did. In 1945 however there was a great deal of Soviet criticism, especially of this country, over the supposed formation of a Western bloc against the Soviet Union which was quite untrue. At that time we had not even had a meeting with our Western Allies to discuss the matter and yet daily this criticism was poured out on the radio and in *Pravda* and the rest of it a constant repetition. . . .

In 1946 I communicated to Mr. Molotov our intention of entering into negotiations for an Anglo-French treaty, Mr. Molotov expressed interest and asked to be kept informed. He made no comment. I kept him fully informed about the treaty of Dunkirk. I have had no communication since, about that matter. When the European recovery proposal was put forward in the same spirit it was offered to the whole of Europe including Russia. There were no grounds therefore for the fear that it was to be directed against the Soviet Union or used for any ulterior purpose. So clear was it that it was intended for the whole of Europe that in Poland we know that even the Communist party were anxious to participate. So they were in Hungary and Roumania and Czechoslovakia even announced her intention to accept the invitation. About Jugoslavia and Bulgaria I never had any precise information; eventually all these states were ordered to abstain. What about sovereignty? We took no step to advise, we merely sent out our invitation for people to answer and come freely if they wished to. If they did not we knew they were not staying away of their own volition.

 . . . At first I was reasonably hopeful that every one including Russia would play their part in this great offer. . . .

In the course of the discussions in Paris there came a change as it was decided by the Soviet Union (and I have very good grounds for accepting this) that rather than risk the generosity of the United States penetrating Eastern Europe and Europe itself joining in a great cooperative movement, the Soviet Union preferred to risk the Western plan or Western union, that is to say they risked the creation of a possible organism in the West. My further opinion is that they thought they could wreck or intimidate Western Europe by political upsets, economic chaos, and even revolutionary methods.

What Mr. Molotov said at Paris to Mr. Bidault and myself on the last day when we were there was that if we proceeded with this plan it would be bad for both of us, particularly for France. As the discussions went forward since the Paris Conference last June, we knew almost the precise dates as to when these troubles were going to take place and when these upsets were likely to occur. . . .

Now we have to face a new situation. In this it is impossible to move as quickly as we would wish. We are dealing with nations which are free to take their own decisions. It is easy enough to draw up a blueprint for a united Western Europe and to construct neat looking plans on paper. While I do not wish to discourage the work done by voluntary political organizations in advocating ambitious schemes for European recovery, I must say that it is a much slower and harder job to work out a practical programme which takes into account the realities which face us, and I am afraid that it will have to be done a step at a time. But surely all these developments which I have been describing point to the conclusion that the free nations of Western Europe must now draw closely together. How much these countries have in common. Our sacrifices in the war, our hatred of injustice and oppression, our party democracy, our striving for economic rights and our conception and love of liberty are common among us all. Our British approach, of which my Right Honorable Friend the Prime Minister spoke recently, is based on principles which also appeal deeply to the overwhelming mass of the peoples of Western Europe. I believe the time is ripe for a consolidation of Western Europe. First in this context we think of the people of France. Like all old friends we have our differences from time to time, but I doubt whether ever before in our history there has been so much underlying goodwill and respect between the two peoples as now. We have a firm basis of cooperation in the Treaty of Dunkirk, we are partners in the European Recovery Programme, and I would also remind the House of the useful and practical work being done by the Anglo-French Economic Committee. Through this Committee we have already succeeded in helping one another in our economic difficulties, though at first to tell the truth neither of us had very much with which to help the other. But it was useful and the work it did was useful at a very critical moment. We are not now proposing a formal political union with France as has sometimes been suggested but we shall maintain the closest possible contact and work for ever closer unity between the two nations.

The time has come to find ways and means of developing our relations with the Benelux countries. I mean to begin talks with those countries in close accord with our French Allies. I have to inform the House that yesterday our representatives in Brussels, the Hague and Luxembourg were instructed to propose such talks in concert with their French colleagues. I recall that after I signed the Dunkirk Treaty on my way through Brussels to Moscow I was asked by a newspaper correspondent, "What about a treaty with other countries including Belgium?" My reply was—I will quote it—"I hope to sign a similar one with Belgium and with all our good neighbors in the West. The Labor Government will do everything possible to prevent misunderstandings arising from which aggressions might result. You have suffered from two wars, you have twice been occupied in two wars and England has twice had to fight very hard. Great Britain is still conscious of the great role she has to play. She will do everything possible to prevent a new conflict in the West whether it will come from Germany or elsewhere."

I hope that treaties will thus be signed with our near neighbors, the Benelux countries, making with our treaty with France an important nucleus in Western Europe, but we have then to go beyond the circle of our immediate neighbors. We shall have to consider the question of associating other historic members of European civilization including the new Italy, in this great conception. Their eventual participation is of course no less important than that of countries with which, if only for geographical reasons, we must deal first. We are thinking now of Western Europe as a unit. . . .

To conclude, His Majesty's Government have striven for the closer consolidation and economic development and eventually for the spiritual unity of Europe as a whole, but as I have said in Eastern Europe we are presented with a fait accompli. No one there is free to speak or think or to enter into trade or other arrangements of his own free will. The sovereignty of the Eastern European nations is handicapped. What of the West? Neither we nor the United States nor France is going to approach Western Europe on this basis. It is not in keeping with the spirit of Western civilization and if we are to have an organism in the West it must be a spiritual union. While no doubt there must be treaties or at least understandings the union must primarily be a fusion derived from the basic freedoms and ethical principles for which we all stand. It must be on terms of equality and it must contain all the elements of freedom for which we all stand. It is the goal we are now trying to reach. It cannot be written down in a rigid thesis or in a directive. It is more of a brotherhood and less of a rigid system.

In spite of criticism levelled at her, Europe has done an amazing job since the end of the war. One has to be conversant with it to understand just what it has been like with all the economic confusion which was involved everywhere. The countries of Europe are returning now to established law and order. There had never been a war like this before. Never had it been so difficult to make peace. It is not a question of sitting down together as it was at Versailles and then at the end signing a treaty. This time it is systems, conceptions and ideologies which are in conflict. I do not want to take an irrevocable step which will make future generations pay just because I was over anxious to gain a settlement for settlement's sake. This time it has to be a real settlement which lasts for a long time.

In this new settlement Germany, like all other European nations, must find her place, but as I have said she must not come before her recent victims. As other nations settle down, Germany can settle down but she must be prevented from becoming aggressive again. We shall welcome her return as a democratic nation. . . .

Despite all the artificial barriers set up and the propaganda blared out, which no doubt will increase after this debate, we shall pursue a course which will seek to re-unite Europe. If the present division of Europe continues it will be by the act and the will of the Soviet Government, but such a division would be inconsistent with the statements of the highest Soviet authorities and of Stalin himself. He told Mr. Stassen in Moscow, last April, that for collaboration it is not requisite that people should have an identical system. Similar statements have been made on other occasions. We have always tried and we are still trying to cooperate with the peoples of Eastern Europe on this basis although the activities of the Cominform like those of its predecessor the Cominterm afford the greatest hindrance to mutual confidence and understanding. However we shall not be diverted by threats of propaganda or fifth column methods from our aim of uniting by trade, social, cultural, and all other contacts those nations of Europe and of the world who are ready and able to cooperate. The speed of our recovery and the success of our achievements will be the answer to all attempts to divide the peoples of the world into hostile camps. . . .

JEAN MONNET

The Value of Common Institutions

Jean Monnet (born 1888), French economist and diplomat with extensive experience in international organizations and agencies, is one of the leading European exponents of a United States of Europe. Monnet initiated national planning for the reconstruction and modernization of the French economy at the end of the war. He was an early proponent of Franco-German rapprochement through the Schuman Plan for which he was largely responsible; he then helped draft the statute of the European Coal and Steel Community and served as the first president of its High Authority from 1952 to 1955. Monnet subsequently organized and became the first president of the Action Committee for a United States of Europe, which, despite its unofficial character, was nevertheless instrumental in the practical development of both Euratom and the E.E.C.

[W]E ARE IN A WORLD OF RAPID CHANGE, in which men and nations must learn to control themselves in their relations with others.

To my mind, this can only be done through institutions.

Human nature does not change, but when people accept the same rules and the same institutions to make sure that they are applied, their behavior towards each other changes. This is the process of civilization itself.

From Jean Monnet, Speech delivered at Dartmouth College, Hanover, New Hampshire (June 11, 1961). It may be found in *Vital Speeches of the Day,* Vol. 27, No. 19 (July 15, 1961).

You yourselves know the importance of institutions from your own history. The thirteen States would not have won the War of Independence had they tried to fight it separately. After the war, the Confederation was only a few years old when you found it necessary to draft a federal constitution to keep the Union together and make it effective.

Since the war, we in Europe have also learnt the need of common institutions.

After the war, it seemed the nations of Europe might be doomed to irretrievable decline. With Germany still occupied, everyone was in doubt as to the future relations between victors and vanquished. Had the traditional relations between France and Germany been maintained, their desire to dominate each other would have led to new disasters. Had either, driven by mistrust of her neighbor, been tempted to veer between East and West, that would have been the end of the free nations in Europe, and in consequence, of the West.

You must realize that we, in Europe, have had, and still have, a far greater problem than you. For when you began, you were basically the same people, with the same language and the same traditions; and you had just fought together in the common cause of independence. Europe, on the other hand, is made up of separate nations with different traditions, different languages and different civilizations; and the nation states have behind them a long past of mutual rivalries and attempts at domination.

Your people created institutions while they were all citizens of one nation. We in Europe, are engaged in the process of creating common institutions between states and people which have been opposed to each other for centuries.

What a contrast their history makes with the way you have grown in the last 170 years! Under your federal institutions, you have been able to develop the most industrialized society in the world; and to assimilate people from all the nations of Europe in the society and give them high and constantly growing standards of living. Thus, your continent has become a nation. During the same years, the European nations have developed their highly industrialized societies separately and often against one another, each nation producing deeply rooted national administrations.

Common institutions were the only way to overcome these profound factors of divisions and give Europe the same chances of harmonious development America had. It is for these reasons that in 1950, when France decided to transform its relations with Germany, it proposed to pool what were then the two countries' basic resources, coal and steel, under common institutions open to any other free European countries willing to join them.

While the Coal and Steel Community in itself was a technical step, its new procedures, under common institutions, created a silent revolution in men's minds. France and Germany, in particular, have been reconciled after three great wars, in 1870, in 1914 and again in 1940. Think of the extraordinary change shown by the fact that, today, at French invitation, German troops train on French soil.

So, the progress towards unity is steadily gathering way. The Coal and Steel Community has made possible Euratom, the Common Market and economic union; now economic union, in turn, creates the demand for a political union and a common currency.

Today, a uniting Europe can look to the future with renewed confidence. The Common Market, with 170 million people—and if, as I hope and believe, Britain and other countries soon join it, it will number greatly over 200 million—commands resources that are comparable with yours and those of Russia.

Further, the Six countries of the Common Market, Belgium, France, Germany, Italy, Luxembourg and Holland, have decided to go beyond the economic union they are creating and to define their foreign and other policies together. Europe today has the prospect of becoming, with the United States, Russia and China, one of the great forces fashioning tonorrow's world.

What is the lesson of these successes?—First, [of] your success in building up the United States of America with consequences which have changed world history. And now, [of] Europe's success in wresting a new future from a prospect which, at the end of the war, was as depressing as that of the Greek city states in decline.

The lesson, I think, is the extraordinary transforming power of common institutions.

Almost every time, since the war, that the countries of the West have tried to settle their problems separately, they have suffered reverses. But when they have moved together, they have opened up new opportunities for themselves.

The reason for this is that, today, all our major problems go beyond national frontiers. The issues raised by nuclear weapons, the underdeveloped areas, the monetary stability of our countries and even their trade policies, all require joint action by the West. What is necessary is to move towards a true Atlantic Community in which common institutions will be increasingly developed to meet common problems.

We must, naturally, move step by step towards such an immense objective. The pioneer work has already been undertaken by the unification of Europe. It is already creating the necessary ferment of change in the West as a whole.

Britain is gradually coming to the conclusion that it should join the general movement towards European unity and the Common Market. As for your country, the prospect of a strong, united Europe emerging in Europe from the traditional divisions of the Continent, has convinced it that a partnership between Europe and the United States is necessary and possible. The United States is already using the new Atlantic economic organization, the Organization for Economic Cooperation and Development, of which it is a member along with Canada and the European nations, as the vehicle of its increasing awareness of interdependence with Europe.

That we have begun to cooperate on these affairs at the Atlantic level is a great step forward. It is evident that we must soon go a good deal further towards an Atlantic Community.

The creation of a united Europe brings this nearer by making it possible for America and Europe to act as partners on an equal footing.

I am convinced that ultimately, the United States too will delegate powers of effective action to common institutions, even on political questions.

Just as the United States in their own days found it necessary to unite, just as Europe is now in the process of uniting, so the West must move towards some kind of union.

This is not an end in itself. It is the beginning on the road to the more orderly world we must have if we are to escape destruction.

The partnership of Europe and the United States should create a new force for peace. . . .

I believe that the crucial step is to make clear that the West is determined not only to complete the unification process, but also to build firmly the institutional foundations of that unity. As this determination appears clear, then the world will react to the trend. We must, therefore, take the first step quickly.

In the past, there has been no middle ground between the jungle law of nations, and the utopia of international concord. Today, the methods of unification developed in Europe show the way. As we can see from American and British reactions to European unity, one change on the road to collective responsibility brings another. The chain reaction has only begun. We are starting a process of continuous reform which can alter tomorrow's world more lastingly than the principles of revolution so wide-spread outside the West.

Naturally, progress will not go without danger: no great change is effected without effort and setbacks. In Europe, the movement to unity has overcome many such troubles and, in my opinion, is already irreversible.

In this connection, I would like to leave you by telling the story of a statesman who was once asked the secret of his success. He replied that in his youth, he had met God in the desert and that God had revealed to him the attitude that was essential to any great achievement. What God had said was this: "For me all things are means to my end—even the obstacles."

II

The Continuing Issues of Disunity

BRITAIN AND THE CONTINENT

CAROL EDLER BAUMANN

The Rationale for Close Association

The author, Associate Professor of Political Science at The University of Wisconsin-Milwaukee and Director of the Institute of World Affairs of University Extension and UWM, studied at the London School of Economics and Political Science (University of London) and wrote her Ph.D. thesis there on "Britain and the Concept of European Union." The article from which this excerpt is drawn, "Britain Faces Europe," was based upon that research. She has also published a monograph on Political Cooperation in NATO.

ONCE AGAIN the British government has been engaged in the re-examination of its policies toward the European continent. Just as the failure of the abortive European Defense Community provoked the British initiative for a Western European Union in 1954, so the proposal for a common market brought forth the British counter-plan for an industrial free trade area. When the six nations comprising the continental community . . . ratified and implemented the treaty

From Carol Edler Baumann, "Britain Faces Europe." Reprinted with permission from the *Political Science Quarterly*, September, 1959, Vol. LXXIV, No. 3, pp. 351–353, 364–369, 370–371.

establishing a European Economic Community among themselves, the British government turned its attention somewhat more seriously to the promotion of a free trade area. It has regarded such a project primarily as a means of associating the United Kingdom with these newest continental developments.

The problem of European Union, of course, has long been a thorn in the lion's paw. The basic dilemma has seldom appeared to the British as one of simple alternatives, however, and they have posed the question "to join or not to join" less often than such queries as "how far?" and "in what way?" Refusing to grasp the nettle of participation, Britain has preferred thus far gingerly to tread her chosen path of "close association." . . .

To understand this concept of close association and how it has evolved, it may be helpful and perhaps even necessary to review and analyze the principal factors which have influenced British policies toward Europe in the post-war years. . . .

With regard to political union in general, no British government, Conservative or Labour, has seriously contemplated British membership and/or submergence in a European federation. The argument that Britain should not surrender the ultimate decisions of foreign policy or economic affairs to any organization or parliamentary body which she could neither control nor veto has been generally accepted and, in fact, was never earnestly challenged by responsible opinion. In the field of economics the government has shown a marked preference for intergovernmental cooperation as distinct from supranational control. Finally, although Britain has become increasingly bound to the continent in strategy and defense, her military commitments have nonetheless been limited by extra-European considerations.

These policies have been determined more by the exigencies of the period and by the practical needs of each situation than by general doctrinal considerations. Yet it is possible to isolate three recurring factors which have influenced the attitudes expressed in the policies finally adopted: namely, the Commonwealth and Empire, the Atlantic Alliance and national sovereignty. These three concepts —in essence and in myth—have served both as reasons and excuses for particular British policies toward the European continent in the post-war period. Their importance has depended not only on their objective merit in terms of the national interest, however that might be determined, but also on their subjective appeal to ministers and statesmen as well as to the public at large.

Hence, the "mystique" of the Empire—the myth surrounding it— has been just as real, and certainly as important psychologically, as the political and economic commitments of the Commonwealth. Much the same may be said of the Atlantic Alliance and British sovereignty. The British belief that Britain stands in a special relationship to the United States and exerts a unique influence over Washington has supplemented the realization that Britain is dependent on the American military commitment in Western Europe. In both respects, the Atlantic has afforded a countervailing attraction to the geographic pull of the continent. As for sovereignty, the British government, as most of its contemporaries, has maintained the legal fiction of national independence in foreign affairs, while recognizing the actual limitations on that independence. The legal theory of sovereignty, however, has at times been mistaken for a political reality, especially in Britain's relations with her European neighbors. With regard to all three of these concepts, then, the beliefs and feelings surrounding them have exerted almost as much influence on governmental policies as (and sometimes more than) the realities they represent. . . .

What light does this background shed on the problems which the creation of the European Economic Community has raised for Britain and on the policies through which she has attempted to solve them? . . .

As with the E.C.S.C. and the E.D.C., full participation in the European common market was regarded with particular uneasiness because of its possible implications for the political and economic sovereignty of its members. The nagging suspicion that a common market of the six would display the supranational tendencies of the Coal and Steel Community reinforced the more obvious objections to British participation in it: the threat to protected and/or inefficient industries, the fear of all forms of unfair competition, the supposed threat to wages and general living standards, the possibility of large-scale immigration and the whole problem of political control. Especially important for Britain was the reasoned belief that because British membership in a European customs union would not allow the continuation of preferential treatment in the British market for Commonwealth goods as against continental goods, it would also spell the end of Imperial Preference in Commonwealth markets for British goods. Despite all this, however, the arguments against complete isolation from the common market proved to be even more overwhelming, and "association" appeared once again as a compromise solution. The principal motivation behind the British move for association has not been the positive desire for benefits, but the negative force of fear.

On an economic level, the argument ran somewhat as follows: When the common market is finally established, British exports to any country within that market will have to face the common tariff. Similar goods produced by any member country will be able to enter any other member country duty-free. The duty on British exports to the union would increase their price in relation to duty-free continental goods, and competition under such conditions would be extremely unfavorable to British goods. It was also argued, but somewhat less convincingly, that the advantages of a large home market would allow the members of the common market to pursue methods of mass production and specialization of labor that would permit them to compete in non-European markets at prices lower than those offered by countries (that is, Britain) which could not engage in similar procedures. Another negative inducement to British association was the argument that if Britain did not associate with the common market it would probably fall under the economic and political domination of Germany, the strongest member of the group. This had also served as the French plea for British participation in the European Defense Community. Economically, British manufacturers have already felt the pressure of German competition to an ever increasing extent and could see few prospects for British exports to a European market in which they would have to face German competition under the conditions mentioned above. Politically as well, Britain can hardly regard with equanimity an upsurge of German influence on the continent of Europe when the whole history of her European policy has recorded her numerous efforts to prevent the domination of that continent by any single Power.

On the political level, the common market proposals resurrected the old question of the leadership of Europe. The "pro-Europeans" in Britain have often argued that the British government abdicated the political leadership of Europe by its hesitant policies toward the post-war proposals for European Union—the Council of Europe, the Schuman Plan, the European Army. They maintained that the continental countries of Western Europe had again and again urged Britain to assume the lead in the movement for closer union but that Britain, obsessed by the importance of her overseas ties and interests and failing to recognize a correspondingly vital interest in her nearest neighbors across the channel, had refused the offer. It was then that the six had decided to "go it alone." This argument was . . . revived and applied to the question of association with the common market. The common market was, after all, not only an economic venture but a political reassertion by the six of their faith in the cause of European integration which had been so severely damaged by the failure of E.D.C. The new Western European Union had not succeeded in winning their enthusiasm as an embodiment of the "European Idea" or even as the proper institution through which to advance toward it. But the common market and Euratom— the progeny of Messina—were regarded as successors to the European Coal and Steel Community, that one notable success of integration on a European scale. As such they acquired an almost symbolic significance as the latest manifestations of the movement for European Union.

This attitude was so prevalent on the continent that if Britain had openly opposed the scheme, her action might have been re- garded there as opposition to the very idea of European unity. The political implications of this were quite clear. If British opposition to the common market had prevented the creation of that market, it might have destroyed not only a scheme for the abolition of European tariffs, but the very concept of European Union out of which that scheme had grown. It might even have affected Western European cooperation in the wider organizations of the O.E.E.C. and W.E.U. If, however, as has happened, British opposition did not hinder the development of the common market, it might nonetheless have resulted in the final abnegation of British influence in the counsels of the six. It was feared that the six might achieve such a degree of economic integration and political union among themselves as to form a continental bloc of greater economic strength and political influence than Britain herself. Moreover, Britain retained the lingering suspicion that a continental union might develop, not as an adjunct of the greater Atlantic Alliance, but as a neutral bloc or non-committed area. It was partly this thought which provoked the view that Britain should assume the lead herself, participate in the negotiations and shape the common market proposals in such a way as to answer both the aspirations for union among the six and the concrete interests of Europe as a whole. According to such an analysis, Britain's rôle in the economic field as in the political would be to reconcile "Big Europe" and "Little Europe" within the wider compass of the Western Alliance.

British policy was thus faced with a double dilemma: (1) to avoid the disadvantages of full participation without suffering the even greater disadvantages of complete isolation; and (2) to reconcile Little and Big Europe in a united Europe without disrupting either the political ties of the Atlantic Alliance or the economic ties of the British Commonwealth. This problem of the common market thus involved most of the many facets of Britain's policies and attitudes toward European Union which have thus far been examined. In the past, the British answer to European Union was found to lie in the two policies of "cooperation" and "association." In the Council of Europe, Britain pursued a policy of political cooperation both in the Committee of Ministers and in the Consultative Assembly and looked toward a policy of association with other organizations. . . . In the field of defense, Britain cooperated in the organization of the Brussels Treaty and defined her policy toward the proposed European Defense Community as that of the closest possible association. With the collapse of E.D.C., Western European Union was evolved as an organization of European military coordination under the over-all strategy and direction of NATO. So also in the field of economic organization: cooperation was the key to the operations of the O.E.E.C., and an associative relationship was eventually developed between Britain and the European Coal and Steel Community. The policies of cooperation and association were thus evolved to coordinate the continental need for unity with Britain's own interest in the preservation of her national sovereignty, in the maintenance of her Commonwealth ties and in the continuation of the Atlantic Alliance.

The United Kingdom attempted to solve the dilemma of the common market by the same formula: though association was regarded as the proper approach for British policy toward the common market, it was given a new twist by the parallel proposal for a free trade area. When it seemed evident that the common market would become a reality with or without Britain, the choice appeared to some as one of simple alternatives—to join or not to join. Others, however, seized upon a third possibility, the compromise policy of association with the common market by means of participation in a free trade area. Avoiding some, though not all, of the difficulties of a full customs union, a free trade area could be negotiated through the auspices of the O.E.E.C.; this in itself would help to dispel any overtones of supranational control. Imperial Preference could be retained as against other non-European competitors and if agricultural produce were exempt from the scheme, the bulk of Commonwealth exports to Britain (foodstuffs and drink) would not be affected even with regard to European competition. If, then, Britain were to "participate" in a free trade area of Western Europe, it would not necessarily be at the cost of her Commonwealth ties. Moreover, such an area would no longer be the limited and cohesive agency of six states but an extended system which would embrace, perhaps, the whole of Western Europe. This shift of emphasis from the common market to the free trade area and from the treaty making of the six to the negotiations of the seventeen clearly reflected the influence of those factors which have already played such an important part in the formation and modification of British policies toward the continent. . . .

In conclusion, it may be well to summarize some of the basic political and economic arguments which have been evoked in British discussions concerning participation in a common market or free trade area of Western Europe. Politically, there was the realization on the part of the United Kingdom that the common market idea had assumed a significance in continental minds as the new symbol of European Union. Outright opposition not only would have been resented by the "Europeans," but might easily have damaged the wider cause of Western unity. Moreover, Britain's association with such a scheme might yet enable her to guide its precepts and to influence its operations in such a way as to provide for her own world-wide interests. Politically and economically, the fear of increased German influence on the continent of Europe has added to the dangers of a policy of isolation. Among the economic arguments for association, the most effective is the admitted possibility of eventual exclusion from a market of continental proportions barred to British exports by a common tariff wall. In view of these factors, the free trade area was proposed as a means of avoiding the Scylla of complete isolation and the Charybdis of full participation by the intermediary path of "close association." Even if the free trade area is completely abandoned, it will not necessarily mean the end of any association whatsoever, for such has been the consistent compromise approach followed by both parties in their post-war policies toward European Union—political, military and economic.

MIRIAM CAMPS

The Decision to Join

Miriam Camps is the author of European Unification in the Sixties (*1966*), What Kind of Europe? (*1965*), *and* Britain and the European Community, 1955–1963 (*1964*), *from which this selection is excerpted. During service with the U.S. Department of State (1947–1954), she dealt with such European economic developments as the OEEC and the Schuman Plan. She then wrote on European organizations for* The Economist *as a member of its editorial staff and subsequently had a joint appointment with Princeton University's Center of International Affairs and with Political and Economic Planning in London. Since 1963, Miriam Camps has been a research fellow at the Royal Institute of International Affairs, London, and at the Council on Foreign Relations, New York.*

DURING THE FIRST YEARS after the war, the British Government, had it taken the lead and tried to create a strong, unified Europe, could have played the determining role in shaping the new Europe —in defining its scope, in setting its institutional pattern, and in establishing its ethos. But, partly because they underestimated the revival power of continental Europe and misjudged the strength of the post-war drive towards unity, partly because they were pre-occupied with other, apparently more urgent, problems, and partly because they were slow to recognize—and to absorb emotionally— the implications of the shift in world power and of their own relative weakness, the British missed the opportunity to create the kind of Europe they later wanted. . . .

Although the free trade area negotiations generated considerable ill will and acrimony and ended in failure, they made an important

From Miriam Camps, *Britain and the European Community, 1955–1963,* pp. 507, 509, 511–519. Reprinted by permission of Princeton University Press, copyright © 1964 by Princeton University Press.

contribution to both these developments: the forming of the Community and the evolution of a new British policy towards Europe. The proposal for a European free trade area was neither as well conceived as it seemed to be at the time to the British Government nor as blind and misguided a proposal as its critics—and not least its British critics—have made it appear to be in retrospect. It was true enough, as the "Europeans" complained, that the free trade area involved no "choice" for the British Government and people. Nevertheless it represented a real and substantial shift in the British Government's attitude towards Europe and the beginning of a questioning of the priorities that had hitherto conditioned all official, and most unofficial, thinking about the United Kingdom's external relations: Europe began to move up the scale, the Commonwealth to move down, and the nature of the British relationship with the United States began to come into better perspective. . . .

However, during the two and a half years between the breakdown in the free trade area negotiations and the decision to seek to join the Community, the views of the British about the kind of Western European system they favoured evolved considerably. The British concept of European unity was still fuzzy and ill-defined but it was no longer devoid of meaning and it accepted the fact, or, rather, rested on the assertion that the European countries should have a relationship with one another that was closer and different in kind from the relationship they maintained with other countries. In economic terms the British "Europe" came to look more and more like a customs union, with some exceptional arrangements, rather than like a free trade area. The "larger Europe" advocated by the British was inclusive rather than exclusive, its ultimate shape was vague, participation involved no immediate drastic "choices," but no eventual developments—economic or political—were ruled out. The approach was a pragmatic, evolutionary one which reflected not only British uncertainties about how far into Europe it was wise to go but also the conviction that it was wise to go a good deal further than had ever before been contemplated. In the British view, there were a number of possible forms for this "larger Europe"—it might be a system in which the Six would fit as a unit, or an arrangement between the Six as a group and the Seven as a group, or a "close association" between the United Kingdom and the Six with a looser association between this inner core and the other European countries. However, in all its versions the "larger Europe" was anathema to the "Europeans," since they felt that it threatened their own construction. Had the British negotiation for accession to the Community succeeded, it would have been difficult to quarrel with the "European" view that acceptance by the United Kingdom (at least) of the Treaty of Rome and its implications was a surer way to unify Europe than the various British alternatives, since it would seem to be axiomatic that the higher the common denominator of agreement among the principal participants, the easier and more rapid the progress. But the way in which the United Kingdom was excluded from the Community and the reasons which apparently lay behind the French veto mean that for the present it must remain an open question whether the looser, more inclusive, less clear-cut, evolutionary process might, in the end, have resulted in as integrated a European system as the Six will achieve, and on a broader basis.

If in 1960–1 an early agreement on any of the kinds of "bridges" between the Six and the Seven or of "close association" with the Six that the United Kingdom had formally suggested or informally explored had appeared probable, it is very unlikely that the decision to join the Community would have been taken, despite the conviction of many of those in positions of responsibility that membership rather than association was in the British interest, particularly once it had become clear that any accommodation with the Six would have to take the form of a customs union rather than a free trade area. However, by early 1961 it was plain that the only effective choice before the British Government for the foreseeable future was between joining the Community as a full member and maintaining the same kind of relationships with the Six that the United States, Canada, and other third countries maintained in the context of organizations such as the OECD, the GATT, and the NATO. All middle positions which would have given the United Kingdom influence over the way "Europe" developed on the one hand and, on the other, the economic and political advantages of participation in the emerging European Community had been ruled out by the combined opposition of the "Europeans," the French, and the United States Administration. And much of the criticism in the United Kingdom of the Government's decision to seek to join the Community—which became more vociferous as the negotiations proceeded—stemmed from a wishful hankering after the unattainable and a stubborn and rather unrealistic unwillingness to accept the fact that the various kinds of arrangement, short of full membership, that the Government had tried for six years to negotiate were simply non-negotiable.

The shift in British policy and the application to join the Community were the product of many factors. But the controlling consideration was the belief that Britain would have more influence— in Europe, with the United States, and in the world generally—as a member of the European Community than it would alone. Although in the summer of 1962 both major political parties tended to turn the question of accession into a party issue, the decision to open negotiations was not taken on narrow political grounds but on broad, long-term considerations of national interest; . . .

Despite the fact that opinion was sufficiently divided, so that the British Government would probably not have taken the decision to join the Community had the alternative of the larger, looser, more nebulous Europe existed, the shift in policy when it came was a genuine one. In the summer of 1961, when the British Government applied for membership in the Community, it fully recognized and accepted the fact that it was applying to join a Community which would—at the end of a transition period—act as a unit in its commercial relations and would possess many of the attributes of a full economic union. The British Government recognized as well that this held many implications for a possible evolution in the political field. Although it was far less ready than some of the "Europeans" to talk in terms of eventual "federation," it was fully aware of the unifying force of a common commercial policy and a common tariff and of the continental pressures for political unity. . . .

Perhaps the essential difference between the approach of the British and the approach of the Six derives from the fact that the Six are more convinced than are the British of the validity of the analogy between the building of "Europe" and the formation of a single state. Most continental "Europeans" think of the new "Europe" as a new nation, a third "super-state," and the forming of new allegiances and the breaking of old ones are a logical and necessary part of the construction. The kind of association that the EFTA neutrals wanted—and that the British Government would have favoured—that is, a form of partial participation, was obviously inconsistent with this concept, which logically excludes all middle positions. The emphasis the Six placed on the need for a "choice" between Europe and the Commonwealth clearly owed something to their concept of Europe as a new state, although other considerations such as GATT commitments and American pressures were also important. Most British "Europeans," as well as the British Government, shy away from the analogy with the formation of a single state and tend to see "European unity" as a pooling of efforts and a merging of sovereignty for certain purposes. Although the British Government, when it decided to seek to join the Community, and British "Europeans" recognized that the process, once begun, would be a cumulative one, and might well end in a new kind of European political system, they were clearly most attracted by that strand in "Europeanism" which sees the building of "Europe" as a part of the process of "denationalization" and a step towards the progressive integration of the West.

From the start two logically distinct strands have, in fact, been intertwined in the European movement and in the concept of "Europe" that has been elaborated by the two groups who have done most to give meaning to the "making of Europe"—M. Monnet and his Action Committee for a United States of Europe and the Commission of the European Economic Community. Both groups, but M. Monnet's in particular, have frequently stressed that what they were seeking to do was to create a new "method" of conducting affairs between states, a "method" which by pooling sovereignty makes nationalism an anachronism. At the same time, both groups —the Commission recently rather more conspicuously but M. Monnet at times as well—have used the analogy between the building of "Europe" and the formation of the United States of America. The seeming contradiction between stressing the analogy between the formation of a single state and insisting in the same breath that the European process or "method" was a step away from nationalism has been avoided in various ways. M. Monnet has frequently indicated that he looks for an extension of the Community "method" to the Atlantic area or to the whole Western world long before a new European nationalism has had a chance to develop and harden. The Commission and other leading "Europeans" have argued—and argued very persuasively—that the route to more effective action on the international plane lies through the creation of a strong and unified Europe.

Nevertheless, although these two strands—the emphasis on "method" and on "denationalization" on the one hand and, on the other, the emphasis on the building of a new political entity—a new federal state—can be reconciled, there has always been a latent contradiction between them. And the drive for European unity has drawn its momentum partly from a wholly admirable desire to find a way round the dangers inherent in the national divisions of the past and partly from a less admirable and potentially corrosive concern with power. Both strands were also present in the British

Government's decision to seek to join the Community, but it is fair to say that the British generally have always been more attracted by the first strand, the Continentals rather more by the second.

Unfortunately, much of the British comment about the dangers that were latent in too single-minded a pursuit of European unity and too complete a commitment to the single state analogy was frequently parochial, and simply camouflaged a basic unwillingness to accept restraints on their own freedom of action. This has obscured the force of their legitimate distrust of a concept which so clearly held the seeds of a new nationalism. The "Europeans" have had one of the few compelling ideas of the post-war period and they have been fortunate in having highly intelligent, dedicated, and persuasive leaders who have not been afraid of taking enormous risks or of mixing vision with reality. Given the essentially negative character of so much of Britain's post-war policy towards Europe, the lack of imagination, the timidity, and the half-heartedness of the few British initiatives, it is scarcely surprising that the boldness of the "Europeans" shone so brightly by contrast that, at times, it tended to be blinding. Thoughts tend to flow in accustomed patterns and the "Europeans," in trying to overcome the limitations of the traditional pattern of intergovernmental action, have tended increasingly to accept another traditional pattern. It is a very open question whether in the second half of the twentieth century the analogy between the uniting of Europe and the forming of a federal state like the United States is not a dangerously facile one. In considering the future of Europe it might be wiser, although harder, to break away from all conventional patterns of thought about the relationships between states, as M. Monnet—although not with complete consistency—has tried to do.

The British application to join the Community inevitably gave a new urgency to the question of what the final stage of "Europe" is to be. The addition of any large power would in itself have changed the character of the Community, and the prospect of the addition of the United Kingdom, with its rather spotty record of enthusiasm for European unity and its Commonwealth and EFTA ties, inevitably made the Six introspective and led them to try to define what it was in their own construction that was essential. In the United Kingdom the application to join the Six set off a much more profound and widespread discussion of Britain's role in the world and of what European unity was, and ought to be, than any that had previously taken place. . . .

The durability of the British interest in Europe is even harder to assess. It is possible that British membership in the European Community was one of those developments which at a particular time appears to be the inevitable culmination of a series of events but which, if it is prevented from happening at the right moment, quickly loses its apparent inevitability. There clearly was a tide which, but for General de Gaulle's veto, would almost certainly have carried the British into the Community. That tide has now receded. But for the last ten years the United Kingdom has been moving continuously closer to Europe and, although the progression has now been broken, it is hard to believe that the trend will be reversed unless the process of European unification is stultified or corrupted by Gaullism. And, at the next stage in the search for the right relationship between Britain and the Continent, the errors as well as the progress made during the past decade may make it easier for the two countries that throughout have been the only real protagonists to find the way to overcome their rivalry and to pool their strengths. The French veto has obliterated with a larger, newer blot the earlier British mistakes in their relations with Europe. More important, there is now a rough parity of power between the United Kingdom and France which did not exist ten years ago. . . . A kind of equilibrium has now been established which, unless the new nationalism of the Gaullists in the end prevails, should make it easier in the future for the French to accept the British in Europe and easier for the British to accept for themselves a role as "Europeans."

K. HEINRICH KNAPPSTEIN

European Union and German Unity

His Excellency K. Heinrich Knappstein is Ambassador of the Federal Republic of Germany to the United States, a position he has held since 1962. He was Consul General of the Federal Republic of Germany in Chicago, 1951–1956, German Ambassador to Spain, 1956–1958, and Deputy Under Secretary of State, Bonn, 1958–1960. In 1960 Ambassador Knappstein was named Permanent Observer of the Federal Republic of Germany to the United Nations, with the rank of Ambassador.

DISCUSSING THE INTERRELATIONSHIP of the projected political union of Europe and the pending question of German unity means analyzing at the same time the interdependence of two political realities—their affinities, their dilemmas, and their prospects—and means also discussing two visions—two objectives which are in fact at this time lacking some elements of reality, such as shape and concreteness and effectiveness. Whether these trends in Europe can go hand in hand, whether they exclude each other, whether they will separate in the course of history, or whether these questions, after a longer or shorter period on separate ways, will merge harmoniously is subject to a great deal of speculation among divergent viewpoints. In any event, the development of both questions will largely affect the future of Europe. . . .

From K. Heinrich Knappstein, "The Projected European Union and the Question of German Unity," *The Annals*, Vol. 348 (July, 1963). Reprinted by permission of The American Academy of Political and Social Science.

The political union of Europe—whether conceived of as a federation of European states or as a "United States" of Europe, but compounding all the essential factors and institutions of modern statehood in the sense of Western democracy—is not in existence. This union is deeply longed for in large parts of Europe. It also may be subconsciously looked upon with some anxiety and preoccupation. Such a union would definitely change the loyalties of the past and present which were and are those of a nation as developed in the eighteenth and nineteenth centuries. The union is still something of the future, the pending but inevitable arrival of which is felt as a necessity. But the union has not yet taken shape and nobody yet knows what it will look like and what his own position toward it will be. What would be its composition in membership? Would it be the so-called Inner Six? Would it necessarily terminate at the Iron Curtain? Would that Iron Curtain continue to exist and to divide Europe? Would it include the British Isles, all or most of the border states of the Baltic Sea, of the Mediterranean? Would it continue to maintain links of association with African states? What would be the relationship, the interdependence with the United States in an Atlantic partnership or even community? Would it be having a hostile Soviet Union as its neighboring country? All these questions concern, with variable emphasis, nations and individuals in Europe, and, of course, these questions are discussed in depth outside the European continent. . . .

Many attempts have been made in the past to bring about a united Europe by means of aggresion, that is "civil war," through hegemony, through dynastical policy, through supremacy of one over the others.

However, only after World War II did political necessity as well as disillusionment about the objectives of national self-sufficiency, self-containment, and supremacy render it possible to work practically on the basis of another, a new concept. The concept of functional integration without political or military preponderance of any one nation in Europe over the others would—if implemented—actually develop a Europe the concept of which is not identified with any one nation in particular. This concept would also preserve the character of nations in the sense that they will not be subjected to the rule of any other nation or national system. This concept actually is being realized step by step. The economic interdependence and integration as well as the common defense system constitute the groundwork for the "projected union." The different circle of nations involved in each of these fields indicates to us that this process has not yet consolidated to the extent necessary for a next decisive step toward political union.

Within the circle of the countries of the European Economic Community—which in the very sense of the term "European union" are the most advanced ones—we also see a diversity of specific interests and problems. One of these countries—Germany—brought into this undertaking the burden and the responsibilities of a defeated and divided country, but it also brought the dynamics of a people determined to construct anew its homes, its future, and its reputation. Another country—France—and some others to lesser degree—brought into this undertaking the responsibilities and burdens of nations with outgoing colonial ties to many a part of the rest of the world which had to be severed and then reshaped in new forms of economic association through a process of national independence for the peoples overseas. With this troublesome task performed, France, Belgium, and the Netherlands—and also Italy—returned home to Europe to build with the one nation in the center of the small continent a lasting and sound structure for a far-reaching political project. Is the extension to these six countries the ultimate with regard to membership? Will the British Isles stand apart? Do they have to be outside? Would the membership for others be blocked pending the definite decision concerning Great Britain? There is probably no easy, no quick, even no general answer. Each of the nations, each of the regions has a particular, a specific profile which ultimately may allow this or that form of membership or association, but, in the end, their participation will contribute in shaping the profile of the projected union, which will definitely be different from each of the member nations' profiles at this time. It will also not be a mere addition of national individualities. In our view, the structure of this Europe now comprising the six countries is open to any nation in Europe under the one condition that the basic principles of the projected union as envisaged at the beginning of the European Economic Community—in particular, the element of integration and the determination to commit the future of the nation to the course of this Community—will not be jeopardized. The legitimacy—political as well as historical—of the European Economic Community's identifying and defining itself as "European" and prejudicing the use of this name, rich in tradition, rich in prospects, is to be seen in the commonly accepted rule that this community is open for membership to other nations in Europe. . . .

How do we now conceive—at the same time that nationhood
becomes apparently less a problem in Europe—the question of
German unity as a vital, as an essential problem in terms of policy,
in terms of peace and security, in terms of the future of Europe.
The question of German unity, in our view, has a number of aspects
and implications, of which some are of a national nature, some of an
international character, and some distinctively European. . . .

The division of Germany describes primarily an unsettled international problem.

To the extent that it is considered to be a problem of the German
people itself, it could be solved in a couple of days, for the nation—
although divided as West Germans and East Germans and West
Berliners and East Berliners—continues to feel and act wherever
feasible as a cohesive nation in terms of common history and common future. It is interlinked, in spite of walls and iron curtains, now-
adays as before, by close family bonds and by manifold relations in
as many fields of human activities as possible. In the face of the
continued international stalemate on the question of the division of
the country, the most pressing point for the German government
and for private organizations as well as for the individual citizen is,
of course, the humanitarian aspect and the determination of the
people to alleviate and mitigate these hardships as much as possible.
However, vis-à-vis overriding international factors, such attempts can
bring about only very limited results, and the tragedy of many a
family remains in the dark, untold and uncured.

On the other hand, the division of Germany as an international
problem concerns primarily the major former occupation powers—
the United States, Great Britain, France, and the Soviet Union.
The German question did not constitute the source for the postwar
East-West conflict, but it was influenced by this conflict to a very
large degree and, of course, influences the course of East-West
relationships.

Also, the division of the country has a number of further implications, namely those related to World War II itself. The mere
fact that this war had been initiated by Nazi Germany must have
had consequences on the policies, preoccupations, and sentiments of
neighboring countries and of everybody to whom the maintenance
of peace in central Europe and in the world as a whole constituted
the major concern in international relations.

The geography, the location of Germany in the central part of
Europe, and its economic and human potential, of course, represent

essential factors that tend to influence if not to dominate any lasting political settlement. Such a settlement has been postponed time and again. It will probably be suspended as long as the Soviet Union has not developed a more reasonable understanding of the future implications and dangers of a continued division of Germany. The East-West conflict has—as of now—not outgrown its life and death implications in the sense that the Soviet leadership dissociates itself clearly from a policy of Communist expansion in the sense of the Khrushchev statement: "We will bury capitalism."

Apart from the immediate relationship of the German question to the responsibilities of the four major powers and their divergent views on the future of that country in the center of Europe and apart from the meaning which the continuing division of the country has to the nation which is thus divided, the question of the unity or division of Germany carries also a considerable weight for the projected union in Europe and the concept of a Europe ever more closely integrated. This might not be visible on first glance to an outside observer.

. . . [T]he projected union of Europe is not limited to any specific area of Europe. It is not true that the "United States of Europe," the "Federation of European States," or the "United Europe," whatever may ultimately be the structure and name for the union, has any natural frontiers within Europe—except in the case of the Soviet Union. At present, it is correct to say that the projected union is primarily related to the six member-states of the Common Market and to those who indicated their serious interest in membership in this community—as Great Britain did and a number of other European countries did who are also members of the North Atlantic Treaty Organization. But . . . there seems to be no major voice inside Europe that indicates a readiness to accept the political, ideological, and somewhat artificial division of Europe in a free part and in a Soviet-controlled one as a natural line of division of the continent. Thus, the division of Germany represents a major concern to all of the European states, because it symbolizes the division of Europe as a whole. The free part of Europe will not be a self-contained union of interest but a union which offers its freedom and opportunities to any part of Europe. This, of course, is, for the government and the public in Germany, a very reassuring element. It is our view that the unity of Germany, in a genuine sense, cannot be brought about by a policy of isolation and separation from the rest of Europe, from their concerns and their culture, but only within the framework of the predominant trends of political, economic, and social integration within the whole of Europe. In this sense, we discern a tendency toward closer ties and identical views also in terms of our specific problem—the question of German unity—among the nations which associated themselves and their future in the community.

German unification is not an objective in any scheme of constructing foundations for another attempt at German hegemony over Europe. German unification would, rather, accelerate the integration of that people in the center of Europe and the common course of European unity. After a long period of expansion into other parts of the world, other European nations—such as France, Belgium, Italy, Great Britain, the Netherlands—return home to themselves, to Europe. These energies—and this also seems to be one of the principles for the union of Europe and for the unity of the German nation—will not be used for the advancement of national objectives but for the betterment of the commonwealth of the nations in Europe, not for the establishment of the hegemony of any one nation over Europe but for the development of a commonly shared and supported European society. In order freely to choose this course toward Europe, a nation should, however, enjoy freedom of action and freedom of conscience and thought. A nation which would have to take such a decision under duress from outside or in a state of domestic turmoil would, perhaps, not be prepared to sacrifice self-interests in a given situation for the sake of the commonwealth of nations united in a political union. When discussing such items and trends, it sometimes appears that one should fear "a return to Europe movement" leading to some form of isolationist policy of Europe itself vis-à-vis the world outside Europe. This, of course, is not so—on the contrary. When Europe has found itself and has alleviated the pressure from the Soviet Union—an element which keeps European nations so much preoccupied with themselves and European affairs—it will, among other things, be more free to look outward to other parts of the world and to share more effectively with the United States, in a genuine Atlantic partnership, the burdens and responsibilities of industrialized countries to restore the distorted economic balance between the various regions on our globe. There is, as far as I can see, no sizable trend in Europe that would favor and see durable advantages from a course of action which would preclude and exclude Europe from the rest of the world. This might have been the case in former centuries and in former decades when the question of union in Europe was conceived mainly in terms of hegemony of one of the nations over others, when a check and balance could not be found or even be tolerated with regard to the genuine interests of the different members of the European community.

In our view, the question of the political union of Europe is not a matter of political wishful thinking but a matter of political necessity, a matter of political challenge which people in our country will not only assess on the basis of present-day implications but also—and perhaps in a much deeper sense than outside observers can perceive—in view of the challenges and opportunities offered to the younger generation whom they want to be brought up in a society of broader interests than those of a narrow nationalistic framework. Thus, support for and policies toward greater European unity are not a matter of *strohfeuer,* of easy success, of easy but quickly fading enthusiasm, but of hard work, of patience, and of constant effort. This attitude will affect each decision which is still to be taken in the national framework and on the background of a national constituency. Disappointments about failures and setbacks do not become easier under such circumstances, but they cannot any longer change the determination of governments and people to pursue this course of action.

As a matter of realistic approach, however, we must recognize that the state of mind in various parts of Europe shows quite substantial shades and even differences of attitude in this matter—which is only an additional reason to proceed with patience and by careful action. Under such prevailing circumstances, the available course of action lies in fact in the field of functional co-operation and progressive integration. In addition, the mutual dependability in matters of defense and economic development between Europe and the North American continent as well as engagement in the rest of the world at the same time demand the development of a balanced interrelationship between these two continents as the major political gravitation fields and as main centers of industry in the free world. This interrelationship has been changing over the years and will continue to change. In this area of cooperation with the United States, which is an essential consideration in all policy matters in Europe, not so much the determination to grow into one integrated union but, rather, the determination and the need for developing mutually beneficial, mutually acceptable, and mutually satisfactory arrangements in all matters of defense and economics and related activities are the immediate targets. The difficulty in this area is that, as of now, it is not one European voice to which the United States is listening, which it is consulting, but, rather, a series of European national voices. This is what sometimes makes it so difficult to arrive at a balanced and perceptive decision. Taking into this picture, in addition, the power relationship of the United States to the Soviet Union, one must realize time and again that it is a burdensome undertaking to meet at one and the same time a number of purposes. It appears very often that a matter under discussion turns into a great psychological problem because both sides of the Atlantic are seeking agreement and understanding on the background of different knowledge and judgment, which can perhaps be overcome through more intense sharing in knowledge, in research, and in intimate considerations which are pertinent for any foreign-policy decision. This, of course, breaks the traditional "sound barriers" of diplomatic intercourse in which one of the essential ingredients used to be the belief that one cannot allow partners, even in a very close alliance, to have a look into the "shop of policy-making."

I am optimistic about the prospects of the European political union—without being able to identify in advance the exact nature of this community or union and without being able to express firm views as to the membership of such a union, hoping, however, that it would be open to any nation in Europe, even a nation or parts of nations which are under Communist rule at present or which are under the pressure of foreign domination, as is the population in East Germany. In the same sense, I am convinced that the question of German unity with its various implications—those of a national character, those of the East-West conflict among the major allied powers of World War II, and those implications which develop in the context of the projected European union—will continue to be with us until the very day that a satisfactory solution can be found which would not be contrary to European and, thus, to German interests. The German people do not view this question as a problem of national prestige or as a prerequisite for a re-emergence of nationalistic, self-contained, and even expansionist policy. For Germany, this problem includes, among other elements, humanitarian fairness to their countrymen. It is also deeply affective of the future shape of Europe. Foremost, however, it is of direct relevance to the objectives for which the free world is standing through challenges, dangers, and daring hours in solidarity. . . .

The nations of the free world, and, particularly, the United States, have a tremendous capital of good will behind the Berlin wall, behind the Iron Curtain which cuts apart one section from the other in Europe, a capital of good will and expectation which has resisted and survived the ups and down of Communist rule over a long period of time. This attitude and this expectation on the part of the population in East Europe await an alternative to Communist rule which is not merely an endless quarrel of nationalistic designs but an alternative of progress in a greater society.

In this sense, the postwar period of World War II is definitely different from that of the postwar period after 1918. It would be a great mistake to overlook these differences. This is something of which the leaders in the Kremlin are very well aware, and they are trying everything to dilute these trends and forces by hammering into the population the themes of revanchism and expansionism. But this kind of maneuvering can be taken in some degree of seriousness only by those who do not live with the generation of this age, not by the common man in the new society in Germany or elsewhere in Europe.

The people of the generation of tomorrow in postwar Germany want their nation to be integrated with other nations in a united Europe. They want this with all their hearts and emotions. They want this for all of their nation in the same sense that they want to keep open this new design for any other nation in Europe. A Europe which would limit itself to preserving the liberties of those who are free and would surrender hope for the freedom of those who are not free at this time would not be a free and united Europe simply lacking something nonessential. It would be a society of selfish purpose. The Europe of the Six is and will be a good and honorable community because it stands by its objective to unite the nations of Europe, not to divide them.

FREDERICK H. HARTMANN

The Problem of German Reunification

*Frederick H. Hartmann is the author of numerous articles
and books on international relations and American foreign
policy and has lectured at the Air War College, the Army
War College, and the Naval War College. In 1959 Professor
Hartmann engaged in research on German reunification
with the cooperation of the West German Ministry for
All-German Affairs; in 1965 he published* Germany Between
East and West *from which the following selection is taken.
Formerly Professor of Political Science and Director of
the Institute of International Relations at the University
of Florida, he is now the Alfred Thayer Mahan Professor
at the Naval War College.*

THE WORLD IS GOING THROUGH a fundamental change. The two-bloc
world is in disrepair; it is not likely to be revived. Polycentrism is
the order of the day as long-submerged national interests reassert
themselves and the national interests of newly independent states
come to the fore. This alters the implications of the German problem,
putting it in a changed perspective for many of those involved. There
is less of the old emphasis on Germany as a prize to be won in the
struggle between the blocs; there is more—although still halting—
emphasis on Germany as a problem for all. At the same time Germany appears to be shaking off a long concern with immediate
material needs and a tendency to allow others to decide her destiny.
Whether the change in Germany reflects similar changes elsewhere or
comes as a consequence of those changes is not really important.

The point is that a new era for an old problem has begun. Germans
are no longer content with the thought that someday Germany will be
reunified simply because its division is, as Adenauer put it, contrary
to human and Divine law. Of course, the fact that the wish for unity

Frederick H. Hartmann, *Germany Between East and West: The Reunification Problem,* © 1965,
pp. 166–174. Reprinted by permission of Prentice-Hall, Inc., Englewood Cliffs, New Jersey.

is increasingly supplemented by the conviction that effective implementation of the wish must somehow be achieved does not mean that success will result. But now that the Germans have shaken off their long passivity it is reasonable to assume that a prolonged lack of future progress will be increasingly dangerous to all involved. There is a tempo in the life of nations, as there is in the life of individuals; when that tempo increases, something will come of it.

What, then, will come of this problem, and under what circumstances are the major alternatives likely to be realized?

First, there is the possibility that the Soviets might improve their position at Western expense, or vice versa. There is also the possibility of some changed arrangement which would equalize the advantages and disadvantages as much as possible for both East and West. Finally, there is the possibility of maintaining (or attempting to maintain) more or less the present status quo.

There was a time when the prevailing mood in West German elite circles was anxiety tinged with desperation. There was the distinct fear that the United States would pull out of Europe and that the Soviet Cold War offensive, as symbolized by the Berlin blockade and the *coup* in Czechoslovakia in 1948, would push all before it. In 1947–48 the Communists were extremely confident and active on the West German flanks: in France and in Italy. The future was in doubt. But the Western response—the Truman Doctrine, NATO, the Marshall Plan—changed this mood and shelved this fear. Only during the period of the six-month ultimatum in 1959 was there anything resembling this crisis in confidence, as Germans (even in official positions) speculated aloud that the Americans would not fight and die for Berlin. Since that Soviet failure to destroy Western unity, the military, political, and economic strength of West Germany has increased, and so has its self-confidence. The Berlin Wall, seen from this perspective, is a Communist Maginot Line; that is, it is not a jumping-off place for an offensive but, rather, an intrenched defensive position.

It is most unlikely that a third Soviet psychological-political offensive against West Berlin or West Germany would bear any greater fruit. Khrushchev was actually deposed by his colleagues for his "adventurist" policies—and these policies included not only the Cuban fiasco but the on-again, off-again peace treaty with East Germany which ultimately began to take on almost comic overtones. The Soviets have no base of support within West Germany in the form of any significant Communist movement. Furthermore, Soviet foreign policy has already entered a period of increased difficulties and complica-

tions: Soviet relations with China will probably not become any easier
as time goes on, and the once-abundant opportunities for making use
of the colonial issue are evaporating now that colonialism is virtually
dead.

Can the West, then, take advantage of the Soviet Union's increasing
problems to force or induce a Soviet retreat from East Germany?
This possibility is also quite unlikely.

The Adenauer concept of building strength until the Soviets were
ultimately forced to make concessions has a fatal psychological flaw.
It is true that nations will sometimes sacrifice some prestige to avoid
war. The Soviets did exactly that in the Cuban Missile Crisis. But it
should not be forgotten that they were not being asked to turn Cuba
over to the West. The United States demand was much more moderate than that. If the United States had insisted on completely humili-
ating the Soviets, it is doubtful that they would have chosen to avoid
war. The concessions a great power will make are governed by two
iron rules of international politics: they must avoid utter humiliation
and an atmosphere in which further concessions become virtually
inevitable, and they must not compromise vital national interests. It is
quite possible to envisage situations in which the Soviets might find
it practical or desirable to withdraw from East Germany. But it is
not at all likely that they simply turn East Germany over to NATO
for nothing in return. To do so would be to encourage other nations
to put pressure on the Soviet Union. The security of the Soviet
Union in the West depends on adequate arrangements regarding
Germany. The weaker the position of the Soviets, when what is at
stake is vital, the more they must hope to bluff through and hold out.
Soviet control over Poland and the Balkans could be loosened under
certain conditions (Poland and the Balkans want more freedom), but
these areas cannot be simply abandoned by the Soviets as a second
step in a Western political offensive. The Soviets would be forced to
try to hold on while their determination to do so would be in doubt—
surely a very dangerous situation for any nation.

So far, the problem has been discussed in terms of a simple and
unilateral Soviet withdrawal from weakness. Another possibility exists:
the Soviets might withdraw if the West withdrew too.

Such a process might occur either very gradually, and perhaps
almost tacitly, or by a formal agreement executed in relatively com-
pact stages. But in either event it would be a program of matched
concessions in East-West troop dispositions and East-West alliance
obligations. And at the end of the process both German states would

be joined in a single All-German government which would be under formal obligation to refrain from military alliances with East or West. The whole arrangement would have to be further strengthened by a European Security Pact which would guarantee Germany against attack and Germany's neighbors against German aggression. . . .

There is a distinct and important difference between carrying out such a plan in conjunction with the reunification of Germany, and carrying it out while keeping Germany divided (as was proposed at one point at the Berlin Conference by Molotov). The plan's usefulness as a basis for negotiation would be completely negated if it envisaged two weak, neutral German states. For one thing, the West Germans could not then agree to such a plan. On the other hand, a plan to create a militarily neutral Germany carries with it greater Soviet concessions than might be apparent. First, a united Germany, whether or not NATO membership were forbidden and armament restrictions imposed, would continue to be a relatively strong power, anti-Communist and pro-Western in orientation. A militarily neutral Germany would not be a feeble Germany, or a Germany neutral in its preferences for one way of life over another. Second, in secret and really free elections the Communists in East Germany would be utterly wiped out. (This is exactly what Khrushchev said about the proposal in 1963—that it would "liquidate socialism" in East Germany.). . .

Why would the Soviets have any interest in agreeing to a plan which, although it took West Germany out of NATO, also took East Germany out of the Soviet bloc and essentially eliminated the socialist framework of East German life?

There are a number of reasons. First, the Soviets currently are threatened with involvement in war over Germany, irrespective of their own preferences. If a new revolt took place in East Germany, or if shooting broke out on the Iron Curtain frontier or around Berlin, the danger of escalation would be very great. The last revolt in East Germany, in June 1953, occurred while West Germany was still disarmed and neither truly independent nor responsible for German affairs. Now active West German forces total nearly 0.5 million, and the trained reserves have reached substantial figures. It would no longer be a simple matter for the West German government to take refuge in inactivity while East Germans were being slaughtered by Soviet tanks. As long as the Soviets remain in Germany, they are gambling that they will not be forced, as in Hungary, to choose between bloody suppression and evacuation. (And the choice they made there did not have to take into account any "West

Hungarian" army!) Nor is liberalization a real alternative to let off
pressure. Competing with West Germany on this basis *would* mean
liquidating socialism in East Germany.

Second, the difficulties in which the Soviets are finding themselves are increasing. The outlook on the eastern and southeastern
Soviet frontiers is steadily growing worse, the inevitable consequence
of China's emergence to power after long centuries of weakness
during which the Russians seized much former Chinese territory.
There is no good way for the Soviets to win the Chinese to solid
friendship other than at a tremendous territorial price. Ideological
agreement or disagreement will not affect these much more fundamental factors in Sino-Soviet relations.

On the other flank is Germany, now shedding her long passivity
and moving adroitly to exploit the Soviet Achilles' heel in Poland and
the Balkans. If the West Germans next throw off the self-imposed
shackles of the "Hallstein Doctrine" (which bars the establishment of
diplomatic relations with any state, other than the Soviet Union,
that recognizes East Germany) and supplement their economic mis-
sions in the area with full political relations, the pressures on the
Soviets will become quite serious. . . . Whether this particular pressure produces the change or not, further similar pressures will almost
inevitably occur in the time ahead. The West Germans on the one
hand are finding neutral states less willing to choose between relations with East *or* West Germany and, on the other, that their own
doctrine hampers exploiting the Balkan situation effectively.

The Soviets have much military power, but it would be used to
hold Eastern Europe only as a desperate last measure, as in Hungary
in 1956. The Soviet advantage lies in the fact that some (but not
all) of the satellite states suffered at the hands of the Nazis, and fear
German expansionism. But with the Germans cultivating relations
in this area, it becomes harder for the Soviets to bring the Poles or
the Rumanians to heel. If Poland became convinced that the Germans would settle for the present territorial status quo, or for very
modest revisions, she would become very restive under continued
Soviet occupation. The Soviets have already found it more prudent to
evacuate Rumania than to suppress the demand for greater freedom.
They might well have done the same for Hungary had not the revolutionary government announced its pro-Western leanings.

There is, in short, already a well-advanced trend toward drastically
changed relations in Eastern Europe. The satellites do not want to
be satellites. Under these circumstances, and in view of the new

German initiative, there is far more reason for the Soviets to make some suitable arrangement for the whole of Eastern Europe. Indeed, this may ultimately be the only way in which the Soviets can gain German agreement to remain without nuclear weapons. This question is now more acute since the tacit shelving of the American-sponsored multinational nuclear force. After all, more direct methods of giving the Germans nuclear weapons are likely to be discussed next.

Thus positive and negative considerations combine to make the Soviets potentially more willing to consider some degree of liquidation of their East European position.

The proposal of a neutral Germany, like all plans, has shortcomings. It would solve the problem for some time to come, but not forever. It would not assure the Soviet Union of German friendship, nor deny it to the West. But it would have the great advantage for the Soviets of severing the West German military units from coordinated planning and training with NATO. Because the Soviets see as the danger of NATO primarily the automatic Western support of a German military involvement with the Soviet Union, the severance of the automatic connection would be highly appealing to them. One might argue, as Dulles did, that NATO acts as a restraint on the Germans, but the Soviets never put any stock in that contention. One might argue that NATO would not act if fighting began between German units along the frontier unless it was clear that West Germany was not at fault. But inasmuch as American units are stationed almost on the frontier, the fighting would probably escalate long before anyone could prove or disprove where the guilt lay.

In such an agreement, the Soviets would lose an advance position and a socialist area. The West would lose an advance position much greater in area than that lost by the Soviets, but it could still count on the pro-Western orientation of the Germans.

Some observers believe this kind of proposal might come into effect through a gradual process in which All-German organs were given responsibilities while foreign troops were progressively reduced in numbers and progressively drawn away from the Iron Curtain. This might be. But whether it were done quickly or slowly, it would ultimately have the same end: an armed but neutral, reunited, and mutually guaranteed Germany which would presumably retain its economic and political (but not military) ties with Western Europe while continuing to carry on substantial economic and political relationships with the United States, Eastern Europe, and the Soviet Union. Such a Germany would have no real maneuvering ability to play off East against West, as some fear. What would be the point, once Germany's main grievance was satisfied? And what would be the chances of any success even if Germany were so tempted?

The last alternative is that the status quo will endure—either because of East-West disagreements and deadlock, or because both sides fear a reunified German state.

Both East and West have a common interest in avoiding a war over Germany. But if this common interest leads them to blocking German unification, they are embarking on what is ultimately a very dangerous course—for all the reasons already given plus the further possibility of arousing German national feeling in some more extreme form. Also, the division of Germany is not the result of East-West conflict alone; it is equally the result of German passivity. Once the Germans begin—as they have already begun—to exploit their central position in Europe, the whole situation may well be altered. A Germany passively tolerating division and waiting patiently for its end is a far different Germany from one that sets out to change things. The lessons of German history are quite clear; they point to the rapidity with which everything alters once the German will reasserts itself.

The re-emergence of Germany in an active role does not mean that Germany will embark upon a policy of adventurism and risk. The signs point instead to the exertion of political pressure on the Soviet Union's weak points. If Germany were to use power politics and threaten to resort to military means, the Soviets might be backed into a corner from which they could not withdraw without humiliation or violence. Although such a military threat might seem too ridiculous to contemplate—inasmuch as Germany does not presently possess nuclear arms—it does enter into Soviet thinking: the Soviet Union considers that Germany has the whole of NATO's nuclear capability to draw upon. This type of action by Germany cannot be completely ruled out if lesser measures were to prove unsuccessful indefinitely. Moreover, such a German maneuver, while extremely risky, might just possibly be successful if a way were left open for Soviet retreat. Some of the inertia presently clustered around the German problem stems from the culture-bound assumption that the Soviets would fight under any circumstances to keep East Germany but that the Germans are not prepared to use force to regain their unity. The assumption is roughly correct at present, but it could in time become incorrect—unless one wants to insist that the Soviets will forever be willing to fight to hold German territory, but Germans will never again under any circumstances fight to regain German soil.

A final conclusion emerges from this study: Germany's division, now two decades old, will not continue indefinitely without grave danger of war. The dangers created by this unsolved problem grow with the passing years. The West has never publicly offered the Soviets much more than an invitation to turn over their part of Germany to NATO and leave. The Soviets, except momentarily under Malenkov, have never offered much more than that the West should surrender West Berlin. Now that the Germans have begun to take the initiative, things will slowly begin to happen; a stand-pat attitude on the part of East and West will no longer suffice. All parties have a common interest in providing for a peaceful transition. Will they be wise enough to find one?

MARSHALL D. SHULMAN

Communist Views of
Western Integration

Marshall D. Shulman is Director of The Russian Institute at Columbia University and adjunct Professor of International Politics at The Fletcher School of Law and Diplomacy. Formerly Associate Director of the Russian Research Center at Harvard, he is now a member of the Faculty of International Affairs and of the Department of Public Law and Government at Columbia. He has written extensively on Soviet foreign policy and is the author of Stalin's Foreign Policy Reappraised (*1963*) *and* Beyond the Cold War (*1966*).

IN DISCUSSING THE PROCESS of integration in western Europe, communist writings invariably put the word in quotation marks, and often preface it with "so-called," to drive home the central point that, while technological progress does create a tendency toward international economic activity, the capitalist system is inherently incapable of an effective response to this necessity. What is involved is not so much the broad, undefined movement toward an Atlantic Community, which Soviet strategists tend to discount, as the specific and practical development of the European Common Market. With or without quotation marks, the movement toward European integration has become a major factor in the evolution of Soviet ideology and

From Marshall D. Shulman, "The Communist States and Western Integration," *International Organization*, Vol. XVII. No. 3 (Summer, 1963) pp. 649–650, 655–659. Reprinted by permission of the World Peace Foundation.

policy. Despite its ups and downs, the Common Market has resulted in profound modifications in Soviet ideas concerning contemporary capitalism and the present configuration of power; it has led to a radical revision of the Council of Mutual Economic Assistance (COMECON)—the Soviet counterpart organization for eastern Europe; and it has greatly complicated Moscow's leadership of the world communist movement. Over the long run, if the non-communist nations are able to sustain a movement toward growth and integration, this development gives promise of leading to fundamental transformations in Soviet policies and in the Soviet system itself.

That this eventuality is contemplated with skepticism in Moscow should occasion no surprise, but there are interesting differences in tone and conviction in the skepticism to be heard at various times and places within the communist world. Indeed, the Soviet assessment of the Western integration movement has evolved considerably in recent years through lively debate and compromise, implicit in the occasional formulations on which the Soviet analysis, like a suspension bridge, is supported. . . .

There are two levels at which the ideological aspects of the European and Atlantic integration developments have been discussed in Soviet writings. One level is concerned with what is essentially a tactical function of the ideology: how to formulate for the communist movement a line which satisfactorily explains the west European developments in Marxist-Leninist terms, and prescribes a line of action for the communist movement—for example, a union of all "democratic" forces against "the Europe of Trusts." At a more profound level, however, the ideological discussions also represent an effort to analyze the major features of the integration phenomenon as a basis for communist thought and policy. In this sense, the question of how to understand the nature of contemporary capitalism involves one of the central columns by which the whole edifice of communist expectations is supported, and is, therefore, of great importance in the determination of policy.

Among the crucial questions which have been at issue in these discussions are the following: To what extent has the process of integration been responsible for the high growth rates in western Europe? How far is capitalism capable of adaptation and evolution (under such names as "neocapitalism" or "mixed economy") that would permit it to accommodate itself to the problems on which the Marxist analysis has expected capitalism to founder? Can there be economic planning under capitalism? How far can integration really harmonize the competitive conflicts between the capitalist countries?

However cautiously and conservatively these issues have been dealt with, the very opening of discussion on questions so fundamental to the Marxist analysis is a fact of importance in the Soviet development. The essential predicate of Soviet anticipations is that the present historical period is one in which "imperialism has entered the period of decline and collapse," according to the Party Program. If this cornerstone assumption is called into question—that is, if the mixed economy of the West does not correspond to the Marxist-Leninist description of the "imperialist" stage of capitalist development—everything else in the Party Program is altered thereby. Up to this point, while Soviet theorists have accepted equivocal modifications on some issues—such as the Marxist theory of the relative and absolute pauperization of the masses under capitalism— they have held to the essential validity of the Marxist-Leninist perception of "internal and external contradictions" which the capitalist system cannot surmount.

The Common Market is seen as a response to technical advances in the means of production, which make possible the expansion of markets across national boundaries. Soviet theorists now acknowledge that this market expansion has been at least a factor, although not the main factor, in the rapid growth of the economy of western Europe. (The argument on this point has been couched in the debate in terms of whether the Common Market is or is not "more than the arithmetic sum of its parts.") However, there is a point beyond which capitalism cannot go in meeting this objective requirement for integration across national boundaries, because under capitalism integration can only serve the interests of the large monopolies. Those who argue that there can be planning under capitalism, or that the state can and does intervene in the economic process as an independent factor limiting the power of the monopolies, are characterized as "revisionists." The communists do not take at face value the provisions in the Rome Treaty regarding the limitations of international cartels, and they regard the trend toward concentration of heavy industry under the Common Market as the inevitable and dominant one.

Despite this "internationalization of state-monopolies," however, the communist theorists maintain that fundamental "inter-imperialist contradictions" cannot be harmonized under capitalism. The national bourgeoisies have their own separate and competing aspirations for power and for markets, and this competition is said to be growing sharper as the "imperialist world market" contracts as the result of the breaking away of the colonies. (One of the difficulties faced by the communists is how to explain the continued high growth rates of some west European countries that have been de-colonized, since it had been maintained that the loss of colonies would be a main factor in the collapse of capitalism.)

Finally, recent theoretical writings on Western integration have emphasized the slackening of economic activity in the West. High levels of unemployment, a downward trend in the general economic life of Great Britain and the United States, and a leveling off of the rate of growth in West Germany and France are cited to prove that the factors responsible for west European growth rates were transient and that the inherent limitations of capitalism, particularly its inability to overcome the disparity between production and distribution, cannot be escaped through integration.

It is interesting to observe that each of these major points of attack—the policy of the Common Market with regard to cartels, the conflicts of interest and policy between the major nations of the West, and the slackening of economic activity in the Western world —is also the subject of much self-examination and concern in the West. The difference, however, is a vital one of degree: when Soviet writers use the term "contradiction" to describe conflicts or problems within or between capitalist countries, they imply by this term that the conflicts or problems are inherent in the institutional structure of these societies, and cannot be harmonized or remedied. The West grants no such fatalistic assumptions—whether rightly or wrongly, history will decide. From the point of view of Western analysts, it is at least premature to regard signs of slackening of growth rates in western Europe as an indication that the Common Market has passed its peak, or to regard British and American unemployment and growth rates as irremediable problems. Moreover, the response of the "Europeans"—the men who are inspiring and guiding the integration movement—to the question of cartels is pragmatic rather than doctrinaire: where and to what extent can the cartels be useful; where do they become a limiting factor?

Of course, anyone committed to a rigid "class" analysis of Western society will doubt the ability of the "Europeans" to exercise restraints upon the cartels—and he would be obliged to re-examine his assumptions if the sources of political power in the West demonstrate the diversity and the independence which Western theory takes for granted. If events continue to validate the Western belief in the flexibility and adaptability of its institutions, the relative degree of sophistication and interplay which has been demonstrated among Soviet theoreticians in dealing with the problems of Western integration thus far may become of real importance. . . .

A considerable volume of factual reporting and empirical data has been adduced in the current discussions, along with the dogmatic assertions. Behind the stereotyped formulations of the written statements, only a hint remains of the range and flexibility of the oral discussions that must have preceded the act of writing; surely it would be an error to take the printed documents as representing the full range of sophistication among Soviet students of Western economics. Even so, the printed record of the discussion of the ideological aspect of Western integration bespeaks at least a growing potentiality for decisive adjustments to bring Soviet ideology into closer accord with reality. To the extent that events continue to evoke these adjustments, a major source of conflict between the Soviet Union and states that do not accept the same premises about the future will be moderated.

From the outset of the development toward integration in western Europe, an evident uncertainty appeared in the Soviet analyses as to whether to treat this phenomenon as a further extension of the American hegemony over Europe, or to consider it as an assertion of European independence from the United States and the emergence of a new power center in international politics. Increasingly in recent writings, the emphasis has favored the latter interpretation. . . .

Although from the Soviet point of view there is much appeal in the prospect of a European "third force," independent of the United States and susceptible to political and military neutralization and economic courting, it began to appear to the Soviet Union that one effect of the weakening of American influence on the Continent might be the emergence of a West German domination in its place. Perhaps, as has been reported, some in the communist world have wondered whether Soviet interests would not have been better served if Britain had entered the Common Market, and had thereby influenced the distribution of power within the grouping. In any case, the actual turn of events has left the Soviet Union with a dominant preoccupation: that integrated Europe may be in the process of becoming a new power center in the world dominated militarily, politically, and economically by West Germany. For a long time, the issue of the revival of German militarism and *revanchism* has been a central theme in Soviet propaganda. Now, however, since the Bonn-Paris Treaty, Soviet pronouncements reflect a new sense of real urgency in the Soviet outlook regarding the possibility of a nuclear-armed West Germany. Ironically, the crisis produced by French resistance to British entry into the Common Market and French insistence upon a national nuclear force rather than a reliance upon the United States' nuclear deterrent power—developments which might have been expected to have advanced the Soviet interest in the fragmentation of the Western coalition and the reduction of United States influence on the Continent—have instead deepened the Soviet sense of insecurity in Europe.

This turn comes on top of a discouraging trend in the realization of Soviet policy: the underdeveloped countries have been less responsive to Soviet leadership than at first appeared possible; the advanced industrial countries have obviously been distant from anything like a pre-revolutionary condition; and the Soviet economic and military base has not provided the support necessary for a strong foreign policy. In Europe, at least, the Soviets are obliged to look further to the future for any encouragement. They must hope that a Europe comprising a post-Adenauer Germany, a post-Franco Spain, and an Italy with a revolving door to the left instead of a window will be more amenable to Soviet appeals for trade and political neutralization, particularly if the momentum toward the Common Market, as presently conceived, shall have been dissipated. . . .

ZBIGNIEW BRZEZINSKI

Russia and Europe

Zbigniew Brzezinski is Professor of Government and member of the faculty of the Russian Institute at Columbia University. On leave as Director of the Research Institute on Communist Affairs, Columbia University, he is currently serving on the State Department's Policy Planning Council in charge of Soviet and East European affairs. Professor Brzezinski is the author of several books and articles on Soviet politics and Communist affairs, among which are The Soviet Bloc: Unity and Conflict *(1960)* and Ideology and Power in Soviet Politics *(1962); he is co-author of* Political Power: USA/USSR *(1963).*

THE SOVIET ATTITUDE toward the development of European unity has been ambivalent in both politics and economics. The Kremlin, unable to interpret the European movement accurately, has oscillated from one reaction to another. Meanwhile the processes of change within the Communist world, intensified by the Sino-Soviet schism, were creating the preconditions for a new historical relationship between the Western and the Eastern parts of the old Continent.

The Treaty of Rome, establishing Euratom and the Common Market, was signed March 25, 1957. It was not a sudden move. Coming after many years of discussion and prolonged negotiations, it climaxed the efforts initiated by the Marshall Plan in the late 1940s. Yet despite this lengthy prelude, the Communist leaders at first seemed unable to perceive the Common Market's full implications, and as a result their responses to it have been characterized by a high degree of confusion and inconsistency.

In the seven years that have since elapsed, the Soviet analysis of European developments, of the Common Market, of the role of the United States, of the reemergence of France, and of the new Franco-

Excerpted by special permission from *Foreign Affairs*, Vol. 42, No. 3 (April, 1964). Copyright by the Council on Foreign Relations, Inc., New York.

German relationship has undergone several radical revisions. In part, these revisions were necessitated by the rapid flow of events. It would be wrong to imply that flexibility of analysis is in itself proof of the inadequacy of the original analysis. But Soviet statements also reveal that Soviet policy-makers were struggling hard to perceive the implications of a new reality which somehow did not fit their ideologically influenced categories.

An examination of the major Soviet pronouncements and, even more important, of the discussions in the serious academic Soviet journals on foreign affairs, suggests that the evolution and revision of Soviet thinking may be seen in terms of four successive major themes, one of course overlapping with the next. The latter qualification is important, because it would be misleading to suggest that at any given point the Soviet mood was fixed and absolutely rigid; within a certain wide spectrum there was a continuous debate.

Thus, broadly speaking, immediately prior to the Treaty of Rome and for a while afterwards, Soviet spokesmen stressed the proposition that politically the Common Market was an American plot to subordinate Europe and that economically it was unimportant. In the late fifties, the emphasis shifted to the political threat represented by Germany (or, as a variant, to the danger of a joint American-German hegemony), while economically the Common Market was seen in an ambivalent light—no longer simply dismissed as an insignificant irrelevance but not yet taken quite seriously. In the early sixties, uncertainty pervaded the political analysis, especially in defining the Soviet stand toward British participation in the Common Market; but economically the ambivalence gave way to at best a thinly veiled fear of the Common Market's impact on the Communist world. Finally, from mid-1962, the political analyses began to lay primary emphasis on the Franco-German threat, while the economic analyses welcomed any open manifestations of "imperialist contradictions."

. . . [T]he Soviets were impeded in gaining any clear perception of the Common Market by: 1, ideological rigidity, with strong emphasis on "inherent" economic contradictions in capitalism; 2, an assumption that old national animosities in Europe would endure, particularly those between France and Germany; 3, a fixation on the American position in Europe and the resulting tendency to judge everything in terms of it; 4, an overestimation of the importance of the failure of the E.D.C. and hence the belief that the E.E.C. would also fail; and 5, a general ignorance of developments

in the West, caused by lack of personal contacts and lack of understanding of dominant trends of Western thought, the outcome of
many years of self-imposed isolation.

If a sense of Soviet weakness and concern was discernible in the
realm of politics and ideology, it was even more clear and also
more warranted in the economic field. The simple fact was that
trade with Western Europe was more important to the Communist
states than to Western Europe, and the development of the Common Market, with its internal tariff arrangements and new internal
trade patterns, was thus a formidable threat. The device chosen to
counteract it was a strengthening of the Council of Economic Mutual
Assistance, a long-dormant Stalinist organization of the East
European nations and the Soviet Union, which had been revived
in the mid-fifties to compensate for the decline in direct Soviet
political control over the satellites. The situation faced by CEMA
was that its trade with the E.E.C. represented a percentage of its
total trade 2.3 times higher than the corresponding percentage of
the E.E.C.'s trade with CEMA, relative to the E.E.C.'s total trade.
Further, while the trade of some of the Communist states with the
Common Market did not represent a very significant portion of their
total trade, it did represent a major part of their total trade with the
"capitalist" world and was a prime source of hard currency.

Because of these considerations, Communist leaders feared the
consequences of lowered customs among the Common Market
countries, combined with the introduction of uniform customs duties
in respect to non-member countries. They also feared that the
endeavor to establish a common agricultural policy, aiming at self-
sufficiency, might affect adversely the exports of some of the East
European countries. Finally, they were uneasy lest the effort to
establish a general commercial policy regarding non-members
might give the business community in Common Market countries a
new lever in dealings with the East. . . .

In public, the Soviet reaction to the economic impact of the
Common Market was to thunder against it as a political and
economic plot. The substantive reaction, beginning in 1960, was to
accelerate efforts to develop the Council of Economic Mutual Assistance. Under its auspices economic specialization has been intro-
duced into several branches of the heavy industry of member
nations; preliminary steps have been taken to establish broad guide-
lines for national economic planning over a twenty-year period; and,
after a long delay, multilateral economic institutions have begun to

make their appearance. The operations of CEMA, hitherto largely an ad hoc body, were also regularized and institutionalized, and a formal charter was promulgated, outlining in some detail its scope and modus operandi. In October 1963 a CEMA agreement was signed, providing for a common bank for clearing purposes, based on a gold ruble (a scheme obviously copied from West European experience). Energetic efforts were also made to create the necessary statistical basis for effective common planning (a matter of particular importance, given the absence of the market mechanism), and several multilateral economic projects were undertaken involving common pipelines, rail stock, communication cables, etc.

The quest for economically "rational" specialization, however, soon proved incompatible with specific national interests in the Soviet bloc, given the wide disparities in levels of industrial development and proficiency. Applied strictly, it was bound to favor the more industrially developed nations, *i.e.* the Soviet Union, East Germany and Czechoslovakia. As a result, the move was opposed by the less developed states, and especially by Rumania, which saw favorable opportunities for its own industrial development. . . .

The economic and the ideological impact of the Common Market thus challenged the basic proposition of the Communists that they have the key to the future. There were political factors, too, which made them pay more attention to the new strength of Western Europe, among them their failure to resolve the Berlin issue in their favor and the gradual reemergence of France as an independent European force. . . .

From a political point of view, a possible Franco-German challenge based on continental Europe represented a greater threat than the American-sponsored Atlantic community. Yet from an economic viewpoint, and even more militarily, it was certainly the United States and NATO that posed by far the greater threat. How to reconcile these alternatives became increasingly a dominant dilemma for the Soviets, and by 1963 they seemed to be somewhat less anxious than, for instance, the Chinese to see the United States excluded politically from the Continent. Instead, they were more inclined to try to manœuvre the United States into a position of joint sponsorship of the division of Europe, in the hope of stabilizing the present partition and, perhaps, eventually creating new political opportunities for Soviet diplomacy. . . .

Russian and American cooperation could maintain the division of Europe, but there would be no guarantee that at some moment

Russia might not choose to exploit European frustrations over current policies of the United States, Russia's real global competitor. For the United States to join Russia in supporting the division of Europe would therefore be dangerous. European collaboration with Russia against America could come about only as a consequence of European resentment of American leadership, due to what was felt to be some American betrayal of European interests. A condition precedent would therefore have to be an American-Soviet entente, based on joint acceptance of the status quo in Europe. This is the goal now being sought by the Soviet Union. Without that preliminary, European-Russian collaboration appears most unlikely, given the Soviet desire to perpetuate its hegemony over half of Europe and the increasing West European determination to challenge it. American collaboration with Europe to reunite Europe and to reintegrate Russia into the Western civilization, a process now being favored by the Sino-Soviet schism, appears to be the strongest and most enduring combination, one in harmony with both American and European long-range interests.

More than ever, Russia is now becoming susceptible to the attraction of Europe. In the past, the Russian attitude toward Europe had fluctuated. On the one hand, there was arrogant talk of Moscow being the third Rome, then of its being the source of a new and universal ideology. On the other hand, there was a deep-seated sense of inferiority to the West and a desire to imitate it. The Russian Communists combined the sense of superiority with a drive to erase the inferiority (through imitation, *i.e.* industrialization). By narrowing the technical, economic and cultural gap between Europe and Russia, the Soviet leaders have created for the first time the possibility of a relationship that is equal and honorable to both. Meanwhile, the Sino-Soviet schism marred the universalist aspect of the ideology, while Soviet control of Eastern Europe not only has diminished Russian fears of the West but also has created a transmission belt for Western values. Without knowing it, the Soviet leaders have performed the historical function of preparing the ground for a larger Europe, but—alas for them—not a Communist one.

The challenge posed by France is a sign that Europe is now looking ahead, is no longer fearful for its survival. This reawakening has necessarily involved a realignment of power in the West, with consequent tensions in the Western Alliance. But the real challenge points eastward. Ideologically, the concept of European unity, with the Common Market as the initial symbol, is proving itself more captivating as an image of the future than a Europe split into conflicting groups as the Marxist-Leninists hoped. Economically, Western Europe has shown a far more impressive development in trade, in the pooling of common resources and in the general improvement of the standard of living than have the Communist countries. In politics, the public debates and disagreements among Western powers have been far less intense and bitter than the parallel conflicts and reciprocal excommunications within the Communist world. All this provides the West with an advantageous platform from which to invite the East to abandon its futile and old-fashioned ideological positions and to join in an undertaking that is also in its interest.

This could be done jointly by the United States and Western Europe in a variety of ways, ranging initially from long-term bilateral trade arrangements (now being undertaken) to eventually a multilateral economic development plan, based on the principle of European unity. Step by step, the East European states should be encouraged to become associated, remotely and indirectly at first, and then more and more closely and directly, with the Common Market. West Europe could also take the initiative in opening its frontiers to the youth of the East—and leave it to the Communist régimes, if they wish, to prevent their young people from sharing in growing European unity. It is doubtful that pressures for close ties, which would be so clearly in the interest of the peoples concerned, could long be resisted by their Communist governments. Resist they surely will, and the present efforts to develop rapidly the institutions and operations of CEMA reflect the realization of the Communist leaders that without a strengthened economic framework the Soviet bloc will be unable to match the West and contain the forces of national self-assertion within each member state. These efforts should not be underrated. But for the time being the concept of a united Europe is still ideologically more appealing and economically more promising. Unless the Soviet Union succeeds in enlisting American support on behalf of the status quo, or unless America and Western Europe fail to exploit the present opportunity and look on passively as the Soviet bloc is reconsolidated, Europe is not likely long to remain "without soul, without backbone, and without roots."

ROBERT R. BOWIE

An Integrated Europe in an Atlantic Partnership

Robert R. Bowie, Counselor of the Department of State, is currently on leave as Director of the Center for International Affairs at Harvard University. From 1953–1957 Mr. Bowie held posts as Member of the Planning Board of the National Security Council and as Director of the Policy Planning Staff of the Department of State. He served as Assistant Secretary of State for Policy Planning from 1955 through 1957, when he left to teach at Harvard. In 1963 Mr. Bowie delivered a series of lectures at Columbia University entitled "Present and Future in Foreign Policy"; this article is excerpted from them as subsequently published in Shaping the Future: Foreign Policy in an Age of Transition (*Columbia University Press, 1964*).

IN CONSTRUCTING A WORLD ORDER congenial to freedom and diversity, the Atlantic nations must provide the foundations. Their own security and prosperity depend on working together on many fronts. Their concerted help is essential to provide the capital and markets desperately needed by the modernizing societies of Asia, Africa, and Latin America. Their strength must maintain the major bulwark

From Robert R. Bowie, *Shaping the Future: Foreign Policy in an Age of Transition* (New York, 1964), pp. 36–40, 47–49, 51, 53, 59–63, 65–67. This selection also appeared in *The Atlantic Community Quarterly,* Vol. 2, No. 3 (Fall, 1964). Reprinted by permission of Columbia University Press, The Atlantic Council and of the author.

against Communist expansion. And only if faced with a unified West will Soviet coexistence gradually evolve into genuine efforts for secure peace.

Together the Atlantic nations can produce adequate resources, both human and material, to cope with these complex and stubborn problems. Their shared traditions and values and their advanced economies provide the bases for shaping the emerging order, if they combine their efforts.

The crucial question is how the West organizes itself. What shall be the structure of Europe? How shall it be related to the United States? The answers will determine whether the Atlantic nations mobilize or dissipate their capacity to influence the future.

For nearly a decade and a half, the shared goals have been to build a strong integrated Europe linked in partnership with the United States for the pursuit of common purposes. These twin aims are firmly rooted in hard experience.

As President Kennedy said at Philadelphia on July 4, 1962, "the basic objective of our foreign policy for seventeen years" has been to aid the progress toward a strong and united Europe. "We see in such a Europe a partner with whom we could deal on a basis of full equality in all the great and burdensome tasks of building and defending a community of free nations."

And the need for a united Europe to be an equal partner was the main theme of the President's trip to Europe in June, 1963. This steady American support, like the European Community itself, has its origin in the lessons of practical experience, experience that had taught the necessity for the Atlantic nations to work together for security, prosperity, and external purposes. Besides defense, in the words of Jean Monnet: "There are urgent problems which neither Europe nor America can settle alone. These are to my mind the monetary stability of the West, the organization of agriculture in an increasingly industrial world, help to the developing countries to speed their growth, and of course, the freeing of trade to be negotiated between yourselves and the Common Market."

Thus the European Community and Atlantic partnership complement each other. Each is essential to complete the other. Both are necessary to enable the Atlantic nations to meet their urgent needs and responsibilities at home and abroad.

This creative effort to organize the West has been under way for over a decade. In that period, as we have seen, much has been achieved toward the long-term goals within Europe and in the

Atlantic area. Early in 1963 this steady progress was interrupted and the outlook put in doubt. The direct cause of the current cleavages is General de Gaulle and his policies. But Europe and the Atlantic alliance are also subject to other strains which he has intensified and exploited. . . .

For relations between the United States and Europe, the current stage of European integration creates serious strains.

As Europe has revived, its people have recovered their self-confidence and pride. The Europeans are keenly aware how radically the situation in Europe relative to the United States has shifted since the extreme postwar disparity. In growth rates and levels of activity, the Community has far surpassed the United States over the last decade. With monetary reserves rivaling ours, surpluses of the Community now contrast with our persistent deficits in the balance of payments. For many, especially those under forty, the Community has already made "Europe" a reality and fostered a sense of being "European." De Gaulle's actions may jeopardize the progress of the Community, but they often capitalize on these European feelings.

This resurgent Europe deeply wants a more self-respecting role in the world. This desire is already strong and will steadily become stronger. In particular, the Europeans wish to redress the balance with the United States. Their present role does not seem to reflect the changes of the last decade or to be in keeping with their relative strength. The sense of being a ward of the United States is offensive to many Europeans, whatever their gratitude for past help.

While this pressure is expressed in various ways, much of it has centered on the nuclear field. With enhanced confidence, the European members want a larger place in planning NATO strategy and in control over the forces for its defense, especially nuclear. The steady growth of Soviet nuclear weapons and missiles has, of course, brought the nuclear issue to the fore. Even so, most Europeans appear to realize that if necessary the United States would assuredly use its nuclear capacity for the defense of Europe. Indeed their confidence that the Soviets are and will be deterred from any attack on Europe leads them to resist U. S. proposals for modifying NATO strategy. But the issue of nuclear control is not primarily military; it has become symbolic of standing or dependence.

The European aspiration for a larger role—for greater equality with the United States—has outrun their present capacity to fulfill it. Despite its potential, Europe cannot yet act as a "great power."

No European entity now exists in most fields, including defense and foreign policy. Thus the new self-confidence and sense of growing power in Europe cannot find an effective outlet; they therefore are often expressed in resistance to U. S. leadership.

Here is the crux of the problem faced by American policy toward Europe at this stage: the Europe which would be a full partner is only emergent, yet the Europeans want and expect to be treated as equal partners already.

Only as the European Community becomes a more cohesive entity with wider competence will Europe enhance its capacity for effective action and equality. Until then, no devices will resolve the stresses resulting from disparity. But, if there is no cure for these tensions, more can be done to alleviate them. The NATO decisions to expand the allied share in nuclear planning . . . are directed to that purpose. The NATO machinery for concerting policy, developing strategy, and combining the two could be improved materially. And the United States could doubtless be more alert to allied sensibilities than sometimes in the past. It will be wise to recognize, however, that at best tensions will persist until Europe closes the gap between aspiration and capability. Building toward equal partnership despite these strains will test patience and faith on both sides of the Atlantic.

For General de Gaulle, the Community offers leverage for achieving different aims. His policies challenge the very objective of constructing an integrated Europe and an Atlantic partnership.

De Gaulle wants a Europe concerted under French leadership, without sacrificing the relative independence of France. Basically he aspires to use Europe's revised strength to foster and expand French influence. Similarly, he rejects the idea of Atlantic partnership, which he depicts as a device for perpetuating American hegemony over Europe. His goal is an independent Europe dealing at arm's length with the United States and the Soviet Union. While accepting the NATO umbrella, he opposes integration of defense forces under SHAPE and other NATO commands. Undermining American influence in Europe will facilitate substitution of French leadership for it. That is why, *inter alia,* he must create distrust of the American deterrent and broader purposes. . . .

The design of General de Gaulle would therefore negate the long-term goal of a unified Europe acting as a partner of the United States for constructive purposes. His Europe would not be an integrated community but a coalition of states led by France.

His Europe would not be a partner of the United States but as independent and separate as possible. It would be unwise to gloss over this direct clash in basic aims. Thus de Gaulle's policy demands a clear answer.

In these circumstances, the sound course is to press ahead with constructing the European Community and Atlantic partnership. The needs which prompted these long-term objectives have not diminished. Not to oppose the efforts of de Gaulle to thwart these basic aims would be folly. It is essential to assure that the European Community is not subverted into an instrument of French predominance, and that Europe and the United States are not divided to the damage of both.

The problem is to make sure that events convince him that his concept of Europe will not succeed. The United States and its European partners are not without means to influence the environment of General de Gaulle. His course seems out of keeping with the basic forces of our time. De Gaulle is, in reality, clinging to the nationalism which the Community aims to transcend. His French nationalism excludes the integrated Europe which would be essential for the independent European role he desires. The other Europeans will not accept French hegemony. And the independent course he seeks for Europe will not serve its interests. De Gaulle's power is negative—the ability to veto, to divide, and to destroy. Given the interdependence of the Atlantic nations, this power affords considerable leverage if used as ruthlessly as de Gaulle seems ready to do. But strong bases exist for concerted action to lead de Gaulle to recognize the necessity to revise his plans.

Whether this can be done will depend as much on the Europeans as on the United States. In the European Community, only the Commission and the other members can assure that the Community goes forward without allowing France to twist it to its parochial purposes. Only the United Kingdom can ultimately decide whether to work imaginatively for future adhesion to Europe.

The policies and actions of the United States will also be crucial for their influence both on de Gaulle and on the course of its European partners. . . . The vital thing is to see that our actions do not enhance, but erode, the leverage of de Gaulle. We must fully recognize the reality of the European feelings which he seeks to exploit and the effect of our attitude on his ability to do so.

The United States will have to do more to show its readiness to work with Europe as a partner. Admittedly this is not easy to do while an effective European entity does not exist for foreign affairs, defense, and other fields. But the creation of the partnership cannot await a completed European Community. Like the Community, the partnership will have to develop by stages and evolve in step with it. As part of the process the United States will have to adjust its thinking to the import of a real partnership. As a nation, our attitudes still reflect much of the heritage of the postwar dependence of Europe. We have not absorbed what it must mean to share responsibility in monetary and economic policy, in defense, in agricultural programs, and many other fields. In short, interdependence, while talked about, is not yet grasped as a practical restraint on our own freedom of action. In the period ahead, it would contribute to the prospects for both the European Community and Atlantic partnership if the United States could convey by its actions a greater awareness of what sharing responsibility with Europe will imply for both sides. . . .

The nuclear issue has become a sort of touchstone in the relations between the United States and the European members of NATO. The NATO actions at Ottawa were a sign of the ferment within the alliance. The various measures—the SHAPE deputy for nuclear matters, the NATO liaison group at SAC headquarters to plan targeting, even the so-called inter-allied force (though largely a formal change)—should be useful in drawing other NATO members into nuclear planning. These steps should be pursued and developed.

But they do not get to the heart of the matter. Increasingly Europeans feel that sharing in nuclear control is the mark of first-class status. Most recognize that the defense of the Atlantic area is a single problem and that a strategic nuclear war would involve both Europe and the United States. But until the Atlantic area is a single political unit, there is a dilemma—Europeans are not likely to be satisfied for the long run with a solution leaving all decisions to the President, and making them wards of the United States indefinitely. If they are to be partners in defense, they expect to share the ultimate right to utilize such weapons for their defense. In practice, it is very hard to envisage a case where the Europeans would wish to use such weapons when the United States would not be ready to do so. But the right to do so may well be highly important in terms of self-respect. The United States, for many good reasons, might prefer to keep unified control of these weapons. But in practice that does not seem a genuine option.

The critical question is how to handle this issue so as to contribute to European unity and Atlantic partnership and not fragment them. In seeking an answer, it is essential to recognize that no solution which is feasible now or soon will fully satisfy the desirable criteria. The situation is not yet ripe for any final answer. Attitudes and conditions will have to evolve much further before a fully satisfactory resolution is attainable. Hence any suggested course for current action will be open to objection if measured by the ideal or by the desires of some protagonists. The proper tests for any proposal should be: does it point toward a constructive solution in keeping with the basic European and Atlantic objectives? Will it foster changes in conditions and attitudes which will facilitate moving toward that solution by stages? Fortunately, as we work toward an answer, the American nuclear umbrella relieves us from great urgency in military terms, and allows time for development. But politically, because of the British and French efforts for one thing, the issue cannot be evaded.

Among many variants, the ultimate choice is between national nuclear forces in Europe and some form of integrated force—either European or Atlantic. With the objective clarified, there is then the question of what practical steps can be taken now to move toward it.

National European forces seriously jeopardize the more basic objectives. They are bound to be wasteful of resources, ineffective as deterrents, and divisive of Europe and the alliance. Of these, the political damage seems most serious. In justifying their national forces, both British and French leaders have insisted that they are necessary for the ultimate security of the nation and to avoid being a satellite of the United States. If that is constantly asserted, it would be rash to assume that political leaders of the Federal Republic, Italy, and perhaps other members will not sooner or later be driven to seek similar forces for their nations. Many Germans say frankly that they cannot accept a second-class status within the alliance indefinitely. National German nuclear forces would impose severe strains on the alliance; but continued inequality will be likely to do so as well. The objections to national forces apply to the British force as well as to the French. The United States has been right in not helping the French force, and should continue to refrain from assistance. But it was a mistake at Nassau to give a new lease on life to the British nuclear force.

An integrated force offers the only alternative which avoids the expansion of national forces, with all its disadvantages. But if it were to be subject indefinitely to American veto, it could hardly achieve its political aim or encourage the future merger into it of separate national forces. In my view, therefore, as Europe moves toward unity, the United States should be willing to concede to a European or NATO force ultimate autonomy without a veto. To do so would merely extend to such an integrated force what was conceded to the British force in the Nassau agreement. . . .

The long-term program to construct an integrated European Community and an Atlantic partnership of equals is a deliberate and creative response to the necessity for shaping a future order. After a decade of progress, this endeavor has reached a critical stage. In the midst of inevitable growing pains, the Community and Atlantic ties are endangered by de Gaulle's challenge to the basic conception. Handling this predicament will test the skill and patience of the United States and the other members of the Community.

The experience of the first decade of the Community provides guidance for the present situation. In 1950, its architects were aware that it might take a long time for Britain to revise its basic attitude toward Europe. Undeterred by that or by the later EDC defeat, they went ahead with practical steps toward their aim. It took ten years of experience to convince British leaders and public that Britain should try to join Europe. It seems clear that no other course would have succeeded in doing so.

The lesson is obvious. In the present situation, the United States and the Europeans should persist in the program to build a strong Europe and a firm Atlantic partnership. That is the right course for its own sake. It also offers the best prospect of confronting de Gaulle with conditions which will show his purposes are not attainable.

This contest nicely illustrates the interaction of the three major requisites for a foreign policy oriented to shaping a world order. The decisive factor may ultimately be conviction and perseverance. But these take on their meaning and underpinning from the consensus on the long-range goals of European unity and partnership and agreed programs for moving toward them. Together they provide the keys to an effective policy.

CHARLES DE GAULLE

An Independent "European" Europe

General Charles de Gaulle (born 1890), professional soldier and military strategist in his earlier years, was appointed to his first political post as Under Secretary of State for War in 1940. In June of that year, when the French Premier sought an armistice with Germany, De Gaulle delivered his famous London radio appeal to the French people to continue the struggle and he personally assumed leadership of the Free French movement. After the war he become head of the provisional government but, opposing the new Constitution, he resigned as Prime Minister in January, 1946, and led opposition to the weak parliamentary system through the R.P.F. (Rassemblement du Peuple Francais). *In semi-retirement from 1953 to 1958, De Gaulle wrote two volumes of his* War Memoirs. *Re-emerging to deal with the Algerian crisis in 1958, General de Gaulle formed a new government which revised the Constitution and established the Fifth Republic with De Gaulle as its first President. In European affairs, he has consistently followed policies designed to promote French influence on the continent. Toward this end President de Gaulle has emphasized the importance of the nation-state, has opposed tight political integration through supranational organizations, and has favored independent European policies in contrast to the Atlantic partnership.*

IN DISCUSSING EUROPE and in trying to distinguish what it should be it is always necessary to ascertain what the world is. . . .

It is clear that things have changed. The Western States of our old continent have rebuilt their economies. They are rebuilding their

From Charles de Gaulle, "The Atlantic Alliance: Allied Comment," United States Senate (89th Congress, 2nd Session), United States Government Printing Office, 1966.

military forces. One of them—France—is becoming a nuclear power. Above all they have become aware of their natural ties. In short, Western Europe appears likely to constitute a major entity full of merit and resources, capable of living its own life, indeed not in opposition to the New World, but right alongside it.

On the other hand, the monolithic nature of the totalitarian world is in the process of dislocation. China, separated from Moscow, enters on the world scene by its mass, its needs and its resources, avid for progress and consideration. The Soviet Empire, the last and the largest colonial power of this time, is seeing first the Chinese contest the domination it exercises over vast regions of Asia, and second is seeing the European satellites which it had subjugated by force moving further and further away. At the same time the Communist regime, despite the enormous effort it has been making in Russia for half a century and despite the results it has achieved in certain massive undertakings, is meeting with failure with respect to the standard of living, the satisfaction and the dignity of men in comparison with the system which applies in Western Europe which combines "dirigisme" with freedom. Lastly, great aspirations and great difficulties are deeply agitating the developing countries.

The result of all these new factors, complicated, and interrelated, is that the division of the world into two camps led by Washington and Moscow respectively corresponds less and less to the real situation. With respect to the gradually splitting totalitarian world, or the problems posed by China, or the conduct to be adopted toward many countries of Asia, Africa and Latin America, or the remodeling of the United Nations Organization that necessarily ensues, or the adjustment of world exchanges of all kinds, etc., it appears that Europe, provided that it wishes it, is henceforth called upon to play a role which is its own.

Undoubtedly it should maintain an alliance with America in which, in the North Atlantic, both are interested so long as the Soviet threat remains. But the reasons which, for Europe, made this alliance a form of subordination are fading away day by day. Europe must assume its share of the responsibilities. Everything indicates, moreover, that this event would be in accordance with the interest of the United States, whatever may be its merit, its power and its good intentions. For the multiplicity and complexity of the tasks henceforth go beyond, and perhaps dangerously, its means and its capacity. That is why the United States declares that it wishes to see the old continent unite and organize itself while many among the Gallic, Germanic and Latin people cry out "Let us build Europe!"

But which Europe? That is the question. Indeed, the established conveniences, the accepted renunciations, the deep-rooted reservations do not fade away easily. According to we French, it is a question of Europe's being made in order for it to be European. A European Europe means that it exists by itself for itself, in other words in the midst of the world it has its own policy. But that is precisely what is rejected consciously or unconsciously by some who claim, however, to want it to be established. In reality, the fact that Europe, not having a policy, would be subject to the policy that came to it from the other side of the Atlantic appears to them, even today, normal and satisfactory.

We have seen many people—quite often, what is more, worthy and sincere—advocate for Europe not an independent policy, which in reality they do not visualize, but an organization unsuited to have one, linked in this field, as in that of defense and the economy, to an Atlantic system, in other words American, and consequently subordinate to what the United States calls its leadership. This organization, entitled federal, would have had as its bases on the one hand a council of experts withdrawn from the affiliation to the States, and which would have been dubbed "executive"; and on the other hand a Parliament without national qualifications and which would have been called "legislative." Doubtless each of these two elements would have supplied that for which it would have been fitted, that is to say, studies for the council and debates for the Parliament. But, without a doubt, neither of the two would have made what indeed no one wanted them to make, that is a policy, for if the policy must take the debates and studies into account, it is another thing entirely than studies and debates.

A policy is an action, that is to say a body of decisions taken, of things done, of risks assumed, all this with the support of a people. The governments of nations alone can be capable of and responsible for making policy. It is of course not forbidden to imagine that a day will come when all the peoples of our continent will become one and that then there could be a Government of Europe, but it would be ridiculous to act as if that day had come.

That is why France—refusing to let Europe get bogged down, becoming bogged down herself in a guileful undertaking that would have stripped States, misled peoples and prevented the independence of our continent—took the initiative of proposing to her five partners of the Rome Treaty a beginning for the organization of their cooperation. Thus we would begin to live in common, pending the time when habit and evolution would gradually draw the ties closer together. We know that the German Government adhered in principle to this project. We know that a meeting of the six States in Paris, then another one in Bonn, seemed at first on the road to success, but that Rome refused to call the decisive meeting, its objections, joined with those of The Hague and Brussels, being powerful enough to halt everything. Finally, we know that the opponents invoked two arguments, moreover contradictory. The first argument: the French plan, which maintains the sovereignty of the States, does not conform to our conception of a Europe having as its Executive a commission of experts, and as its Legislative a Parliament cut off from national realities. The second argument: although Britain does not agree to lose its sovereignty, we will not enter into any European political organization to which it would not belong.

The French plan for European organization not being adopted by Italy and by the Benelux countries; moreover, integration not being able to lead to anything other than an American protectorate; finally, Great Britain having shown throughout the interminable Brussels negotiations that it was not in a position to accept the common economic rules and, by the Nassau agreement, that its defense force, particularly in the nuclear domain, would not be European for lack of being autonomous in relation to the United States—it seemed to the Government of the Federal Republic of Germany and to the Government of the French Republic that their bilateral cooperation could have some value. It was then that, on the proposal of the German Government, the French-German Treaty of January 22, 1963 was concluded, which I had the honor of signing right here with Chancellor Adenauer.

However, it must be noted that, if the French-German Treaty made possible limited results in some areas, also if it led the two Governments and their services to establish contacts which, for our part, and altogether, we judge can be useful and which are, in any case, very pleasant, up to now a common line of conduct has not emerged. Assuredly there is not, and there could not be any opposition, strictly speaking, between Bonn and Paris. But, whether it is a matter of the effective solidarity of France and Germany concerning their defense, or even of the stand to take and the action to pursue toward the East, above all the Moscow satellites, or correlatively of the question of boundaries and nationalities in Central and Eastern

Europe, or of the recognition of China and of the diplomatic and economic mission which can be opened to Europe in relation to that great people, or of peace in Asia and particularly Indochina and Indonesia, or of the aid to give to the developing countries in Africa, Asia and Latin America, or of the organization of the agricultural common market and consequently the future of the Community of the Six—one could not say that Germany and France have yet agreed to make together a policy and one could not dispute that this results from the fact that Bonn has not believed, up to now, that this policy should be European and independent. If this state of affairs were to last, there would be the risk, in the long run, of doubts among the French people, of misgivings among the German people and, among their four partners of the Rome Treaty, an increased tendency to leave things as they are, while waiting, perhaps, to be split up.

But, throughout the world, the force of things is doing its work. In wanting and in proposing the organization of a Europe having its own policy, France is sure of serving the balance, the peace and progress of the world. Moreover, she is now strong enough and sure enough of herself to be able to be patient, except for major external changes which would jeopardize everything and therefore lead her to change her direction. . . . In waiting for the sky to clear, France is pursuing, by her own means, that which a European and independent policy can and should be. It is a fact that people everywhere are pleased with it and that for herself it is not an unsatisfactory situation.

III Looking Ahead: What Kind of Europe?

WHAT FUTURE INTEGRATION: STAGNATION OR SUCCESS?

KARL W. DEUTSCH

The Limits of Integration

Karl W. Deutsch, Professor of Political Science at Yale University, has written several works related to both European politics and political integration, including Political Community at the International Level (*1954*); *he is co-author of* Political Community and the North Atlantic Area (*1957*) *and* The Integration of Political Communities (*1964*).

DESPITE . . . UNRESOLVED QUESTIONS in our imperfect understanding of the economic effects of the integration of markets, it seems that some further advances toward a more integrated European political community will doubtlessly be attempted in the 1960's. Their objectives may seem clear: greater prosperity and economic growth; further progress in technology and the application of science; more security from military threats, both from within and from without; greater popular resistance to Communist and Soviet propaganda; and greater respect and prestige for Europeans in the world at large, including not only Asia and Africa but also notably the United States. What

From Karl W. Deutsch, "Towards Western European Integration: An Interim Assessment," *Journal of International Affairs,* Vol. XVI, No. 1 (1962), pp. 94–101. Reprinted by permission of the *Journal of International Affairs.*

seems less clear is the pathway—or pathways—by which these objectives are to be approached. Are these goals to be sought in the main
by policies of supra-national political amalgamation or by less formal
policies of pluralism?

Among the many suggestive formulations of the sociological theo-
rist Talcott Parsons, three generalizations seem relevant for our discussion at this point. In the gradual transition from traditional to
fully modern culture and technology, Parsons suggests, social systems
tend to rely less on locally or ethnically *particular* organizations and
patterns of action, and more on *universal* ones which are applicable
over a wide range of groups and places. The same shift to modernity,
however, implies a shift from institutions and ways of acting that are
fundamentally *diffuse*—i.e., that serve vaguely a great many different
functions through one and the same organization—to those that are
functionally *specific,* i.e., where any single organization serves only a
single specific function or at most a small group of closely related functions. Still another aspect of the transition to full modernity, according
to Parsons, is the shift from the allocation of roles, expectations and
awards by *ascription*—that is, according to what a person, group, or
institution *is* or is believed to be—to an even greater reliance on
making such allocations by *achievement*—that is, in accordance with
what an individual, group, or organization has actually done in
terms of actually meeting some more or less specified criteria of
performance.

The traditional community, which the German sociologist Ferdi-
nand Tönnies called *Gemeinschaft*—such as a family or a tribe, or a
modern nation and a nation-state—was particular in membership,
diffuse in function, and ascriptive in allocation. It performed a wide
and ill-defined range of services for the particular set of persons that
happened to belong to it and to whom were ascribed, by virtue of
the simple fact of their belonging, the intrinsic qualities which entitled
them to expect the services, roles and rewards which the community
might have to bestow. The opposite of this warm, secure and emotional shelter of the *Gemeinschaft* . . . is the modern, highly rational
special purpose organization, the *Gesellschaft*—such as a joint stock
company, a textile tariff lobby or an international mathematics congress—which is open, in principle, to the universality of all potential
members so long as they happen to share this one specific interest
and perhaps meet some universal test of achievement, regardless of
their own differences. Ideally, such a *Gesellschaft* then allocates its
resources, rewards, roles and expectations on the purely rational

grounds of what seems most likely to promote its specific purpose and of what seem to be appropriate criteria of actual performance and achievement, rather than by any ascription of any potency or virtue to anyone or anything on other grounds.

In practice, to be sure, these two ideal types are rarely if ever found in this pure form. Even traditional communities pay some attention to achievement, and even rational organizations sometimes tend to make use of ascriptive criteria in allocating facilities or roles. Nevertheless, there is a real distinction between organizations close to the traditional or the modern of these two poles, and it is this distinction that offers some food for speculation about some possible alternative pathways towards further European integration.

Up to the beginning of 1962, most or all of the effective and successful supra-national organizations in Western Europe have been functionally specific, such as ECSC, NATO, the Customs Cooperation Council, the European Civil Aviation Conference, and many others. Where new functions had to be dealt with, new specific organizations were founded in preference to broadening the competence of any one of the old ones. Functionally diffuse organizations, such as the Council of Europe, acquired no substantial powers to act; they remained limited, in effect, to the specific function of discussion and advice. As might be expected from the same line of reasoning, the attempts to broaden NATO beyond its specific military function have met with great and continued difficulties. All attempts to give NATO also some "broader" economic, political, or cultural context—and thus to turn it more nearly into a functionally diffuse general purpose organization—thus far have remained unsuccessful. The failure in 1954 of the attempt to add the military functions of the projected European Defense Community and the political tasks of the proposed European Political Community to the limited coal and steel jurisdiction of ECSC—and thus to merge all three into a functionally more diffuse European Community—points in the same direction.

The persistent difficulties with functional diffuseness in supra-national organizations are matched, albeit to a lesser degree, by difficulties with particularity. The particularly European Organization for European Economic Cooperation (OEEC) has been replaced by the Organization for Economic Cooperation and Development (OECD) which includes the United States and Canada, two extra-European industrial powers which meet its specific functional requirements and are clearly relevant to its specific purpose of economic cooperation and development. . . . Already in 1948, the specific military concerns of NATO had required the extension of that organization beyond the particular orbit of "North Atlantic" geography indicated in its name, and had led to the inclusion of such conspicuously non-North Atlantic countries as Turkey and Greece. A similar fate may yet befall the European Coal and Steel Community if the functional requirements of the coal and steel trade should come to require it; and the Common Market is already beset with problems involving the inclusion or exclusion of Britain, the Commonwealth countries, and the African member states of the old French Community. If functional specificity here counsels expansion of the Common Market, the prospect of growing functional diffuseness may inhibit it. A specific common market for most industrial commodities can perhaps be readily negotiated; a similar market for industrial labor is somewhat more difficult; and the extension of the Common Market to agricultural products . . . proved still more laborious.

There is another hidden but no less serious reef in the way of further progress of the Common Market. So long as national tariffs and other political controls over trade between its member states remain high enough to be effective, the Common Market remains limited to the specific function of facilitating freer interchange of a limited number of commodities without interfering substantially with the national political control of each national economy. Once, however, the sector of freely exchanged goods becomes large in comparison to the domestic sector, the national controls over domestic levels of prices, employment, credit and taxation all may become precarious, or even increasingly inoperative. If there were no business cycle, nor any other economic instabilities or inequalities, this would matter little, or even might be good. . . . The matter looks very different, however, if one accepts the continuing need for some national or supra-national agencies of government to perform the functions of economic control, stabilization, development, and the active promotion of greater economic equity, educational opportunity and social welfare. In recent decades the bulk of these services has been claimed by citizens of each state on the ascriptive basis of their nationality, and the bulk of the corresponding functions has been performed by the diffuse and particular community of the nation-state through a host of specific bureaucratic agencies. In the Europe of early 1962, there is as yet no effective political community, no governmental machinery of either legislation or administration capable of performing these functions at the supra-national level. How soon and how effectively, if at all, such institutions will be created in the 1960's, no one can say. In the meantime, however, the official timetable of the Common Market agreement will drive Western Europe toward an increasingly critical dependence on an international policy consensus and political machinery, neither of which yet exists.

The problem here is deeper than a matter of machinery. The Common Market, much like the European Coal and Steel Community, seems firmly accepted by the most directly interested political elites of the participating countries. The support of these interests has sometimes been purchased by the judicious toleration of the old cartel practices that have long been traditional in Western Europe. No less important, the Common Market and the other European organizations like it have all been tolerated by the elites whose interests they touched only marginally or not at all; and they were further bolstered by the widespread apathy, rather than by any active and determined loyalty, of the broad masses of the voters. Being functionally specific, such European organizations stirred up relatively little opposition. Once they begin to become functionally diffuse, however, as they must become when they move toward amalgamated or federal institutions of multi-purpose government at some West European level, they may come to be perceived as a diffuse threat by many previously unconcerned elite groups and by a large part of mass opinion. . . .

Much of the integration of Europe has been planned by its proponents in reliance on some "spill-over" process through which each item of functional amalgamation would generate relatively quickly an acute need for some other step, so as to give the whole process an accelerating series of impacts. In the 1950's, "spill-over" perhaps was less effective than suggested by this theory. Most of the new integrative organizations were set up by deliberate choice of policy, rather than under the impact of any quickly mounting needs or pressures. If such pressures for more powerful European general purpose institutions should develop in the 1960's, the time needed to bring any such stronger European amalgamated or federated agencies into being might depend most of all not only upon the degree of elite agreement but also of broad popular perception and consensus achieved by that time.

Dependable European integration would imply many things. It would imply the achievement of a steady and high level of mutual transactions between the West European countries, eventually even

close to the levels prevailing between the states of the United States
or at least substantially above the intra-European levels of the eve of
the First World War. . . .

In addition to a high level of mutual transactions, the minimal
integration required for internal peace requires a settled unwillingness
to resort to warfare for the decision of mutual disputes and an
absence of any substantial preparations for the specific possibility of
such mutual hostilities. Such minimal integration is attainable not
only within a single country, such as the United States, but also
among several sovereign countries: for example, neighbors such as
Canada and the United States or the Scandinavian states together
might form a pluralistic security community. Beyond this, a willingness to devote substantial resources to long-range positive common
undertakings—going well beyond mere military alliances—may carry
a community of countries to the point of accepting an amalgamated
political community under some form of federal or otherwise amalgamated government; and if such a community is effectively free of
fears of civil war, we may call it an amalgamated security community.

Given a high level of mutual transactions, minimal integration can
be reached and even more far-reaching federation or amalgamation
attained, with the aid of three broad classes of favorable conditions
familiar to historians. The first of these is the operation of formative
events; the second, that of special unifying institutions; the third is
that of the almost imperceptible but cumulative change in the political climate, in the "spirit of the times," in short, in the things that a
new generation is coming to take for granted. Even well before
minimal integration is reached, the "take-off" of the political movement towards integration or union—the transition from the advocacy
of unity by a few prophets or intellectuals to its support by some
substantial and more or less constantly operating political group—
can be hastened by one or more of these three processes.

In the case of Western Europe, our interim survey may suggest
that the speed and power of the effects of the formative events of
1945–1950, as well as of the effects of the European institutions put
into operation thus far, though impressive, may still have been somewhat overrated; and that the next five or ten years may still belong
to a pluralistic approach where sovereign governments in close and
effective consultation are coordinating their policies and practices,
creating and operating an array of common, specific and functional
agencies, and eventually coordinating not only the variegated politi-

cal demands of their populations, but, at a more fundamental level, the habits, expectations, perceptions, and self-identifications from which such political demands arise.

This quiet change in the political climate and in the very spirit of Europe may well be under way by now. It is clearly nowhere near completion in early 1962. . . .

Nevertheless, the quiet process is at work. The climate is changing, and another five or ten years may show how much more ready Europe will have become to surmount what today still looks like formidable obstacles to her creative and lasting unification.

ERNST B. HAAS

Progress of the New Europe

Ernst B. Haas is a Professor of Political Science at the University of California, Berkeley. He has written numerous authoritative articles dealing with regionalism, European unity, and functional integration. His books include The Uniting of Europe (1958), Consensus Formation in the Council of Europe (1960), *and* Beyond the Nation-State: Functionalism and International Organization (1964). *In addition to his work on European integration, Professor Haas has studied the political implications of economic integration in Latin America. The following selection is excerpted from an article entitled "Technocracy, Pluralism and the New Europe" which appeared in* A New Europe? (*Boston, 1964*).

THE PRACTICES ASSOCIATED with regional integration in contemporary western Europe correspond to a type of society and economy variously labeled "post-industrial," "post-bourgeois" or merely "the New Europe." This New Europe evolved historically from the interconnected strands of capitalism, industrialism and pluralistic democracy. It resembles in many respects the type of economy and society familiar to us in North America. Regional government in such a society is thus merely an adaptation on the scale of half a continent of forms of social and economic organization which evolved historically at the national level. Regional government in the New Europe is the institutional and political recognition that societies have changed dramatically since 1945, so dramatically that they cannot be adequately described in the doctrines and ideologies made familiar by nineteenth- and early twentieth-century political thought. Hence the New Europe and its regional government is the future of that part of history which has also been aptly described as "the end of ideology." . . .

From Ernst B. Haas, "Technocracy, Pluralism and the New Europe," *Daedalus.* Reprinted by permission of the American Academy of Arts and Sciences.

[To assess "the New Europe"] the nature of supranationality must first be well understood.

General de Gaulle equates supranationality with a federalism which he detests; Jean Monnet identifies it with a federalism of which he is a leading partisan. Both gentlemen mistake the essence of the phenomenon, even though Monnet is rightfully considered its founding father. British statesmen were repelled by the European Community for a long time because they could conceive only of federal or traditional intergovernmental international institutions, and they held the Community to be almost federal. Supranationality, however, is neither federalism nor intimate intergovernmental cooperation, even though the institutions it employs resemble those of a federation more than the United Nations or NATO. Supranationality is a unique style of making international decisions, unique because of the nature of the participants, the context in which decisions are made, and the quality of the decisions produced.

The participants in the supranational decision-making process include of course "governments"; indeed, governments theoretically dominate it because their representatives constitute the Councils of Ministers which rule the three communities. But these representatives are for the most part high civil servants meeting in almost continuous confrontation with their opposite numbers and working out common policies on the basis of their perception of the technical possibilities inherent in whatever is being discussed. Only exceptionally are decisions wholly made by the ministers themselves, and then only on the basis of suggestions and proposals prepared by the European Commission or the High Authority; that is, by experts whose job it is to find common ground among the six nations. Other participants include spokesmen for all major national and European interest groups, who confer almost all the time with the specialists in the Community executives. Proposals by the executives to the ministers always take into account the demands of the major interest groups. Finally, the legislatures of the six countries participate in the form of the European Parliament, which makes its wishes known and which demands to be consulted by the commissions and the High Authority. If it is still true that the representatives of the six governments dispose, this is so only because the European executives, in consultation with private and parliamentary groups, propose. The alternative dispositions in areas subject to regional jurisdiction are defined and limited by the range of proposals stemming from extragovernmental sources.

The context of supranational decisions is economic, social and technical. But this should not lead us to conclude that just because expressly "political" and military issues are excluded, supranational decisions are somehow secondary. The essence of supranationality lies in the tendency for economic and social decisions to "spill over" into the realm of the political, to arise from and further influence the political aspirations of the major groupings and parties in democratic societies. The supranational style stresses the indirect penetration of the political by way of the economic because the "purely" economic decisions always acquire political significance in the minds of the participants. In short, the kind of economics and social questions here dealt with are those at the very core of the modern welfare state.

The quality of supranational decisions differs sharply from the federal and the intergovernmental norms. In intergovernmental negotiations differing initial positions are usually compromised on the level of the lowest common denominator. That is, the least cooperative participant defines the limits of the compromise. In federal systems simple majoritarianism decides in ultimate situations of conflict, even if this be the majority of one vote on a federal Supreme Court. In supranational systems, on the other hand, the compromise pattern often involves "splitting the difference" between the final bargaining positions of the participants. More significantly still, supranational systems feature a bargaining process which I call "upgrading common interests." It occurs when the participants have great difficulty in arriving at a common policy; yet they do agree that they should have some common stand in order to safeguard other aspects of interdependence among them. Hence they tend to swap concessions in related fields, but outside the specific contexts in which disagreement prevails. Further, the swapping takes place on the basis of services rendered by an institutionalized conciliator with powers of its own, the European executives; that body is able to construct patterns of mutual concessions from various policy contexts and in so doing usually manages to upgrade its own powers at the expense of the member governments. Yet those governments do not feel as if they had been bullied: common interests are upgraded also in the sense that each feels that by conceding something it gained something else. The final compromise, far from somehow debasing the bargaining process, induces a feeling of commitment, of creativity and of gain in the participants. . . .

Few people believe that the existing system of regional government, that supranational method now under French attack, has a claim to longevity. I believe that it does. Because it corresponds to the nature of the New Europe, the Europe of adaptative interest groups, bureaucracies, technocrats and other units with modest but pragmatic interests resembling the traditional nationalisms of *Grosspolitik* only very remotely, it may well be a real system of government rather than a mere temporary style. "There are more things in Heaven and Earth, General de Gaulle, than are dreamt of in your philosophy." . . .

Our argument, however, runs into the very obvious obstacle of active dislike for the supranational method on the part of some Europeans and of their practical resistance to continued integration, both among the Six and between the Six and the rest of Europe as well as North America. This resistance is explained by some scholars as a manifestation of the reassertion of the political function. Supranational integration may well take place on the basis of economic policies spilling over into more and more neighboring fields of activity, they suggest, until the *economic* potentialities of the process are exhausted. As long as we are merely dismantling tariffs, establishing fair pricing rules for steel, harmonizing social security rates and facilitating the free movement of manpower we remain within the logic of the economic spill-over. But once the limits of these tasks are reached, once these objectives are attained, we are up against the hard core of politics: foreign policy coordination, defense arrangements and the ultimate relationship between *national* political planning and *national* economic welfare. When statesmen feel that this point has been reached—as de Gaulle clearly does—the spill-over will trickle away and integration will either stop or take on a purely political-constitutional hue. Supranationality will then be condemned to linger listlessly in the economic institutions already created but foreclosed from further development. The Europe of the Six may be at this point now.

This formulation mistakes the nature of the New Europe. It is not only the outer military shell of nations which has become very penetrable. Self-reliance equals the flirtation with suicide not only in the realm of defense. The outer shell of nations has become penetrable even more in terms of trade, travel, investment, values and welfare in proportion to the degree of industrial pluralism which prevails domestically. The image which characterizes the nation-state as a warm and self-contained community and juxtaposes it to the colder and more calculating world of nation-states labeled "international society" is oversimplified and misleading, at least in the North Atlantic

area. The internal *as well* as the external network of relations of
nations constitute a species of society; both increasingly function on
the basis of calculated interest and adjustment among interests, on
the part of voluntary groups as well as of governments. And the
extent of the adjustment is deeply influenced by the degree of
penetrability which the outer shell of the total national corpus
permits.

Armed with this perspective, let us have another look at the spill-
over process. While it assumes the continued commitment of major
participants to the process of integration, it does not presume passion-
ate enthusiasm and takes for granted opposition to specific items in
the catalogue of integrative ventures. The support for given steps
rests on the convergence of expectations of the participants; competing expectations and goals can be compromised on the basis of
swapping concessions from a variety of sectors, all under the generalized purview of supranational institutions and processes. Lack of
agreement among governments can thus give rise to increased
delegated powers on the part of these institutions. Dissatisfaction
with the results of partial economic steps may lead labor and industry
to demand new central action. Supranational institutions and national
groups may create situations which can be dealt with only through
central action, unless the nations are willing to suffer deprivations in
welfare. The very penetrability of the national shell leaves the nation
open to the lure of intersectorial bargains whereby one government
is willing to take a loss in exchange for a gain in another sector.
Nations outside the economic grouping but deeply intertwined with
it through the activities of their citizens may experience problems
which can be solved—if welfare is not to be sacrificed—only by joining the grouping and upgrading its central powers. No statesman,
even if he deeply dislikes the process, can permanently isolate his nation from a commitment to unity which is already partially implemented, unless he is willing to pay the price in diminished welfare.
De Gaulle may be willing to pay that price; but I doubt that French
society is. Moreover, if de Gaulle expects Holland, Belgium, Italy and
post-Adenauer Germany to endorse certain French goals he will be
obliged to pay for this support by acquiescing to the goal expectations of his allies. And this involves him willy-nilly in more supranational integration.

What, then, is spilling over in the Europe of the Six despite current
French policy? Where does the generalized post-national statistical
mood manifest itself even though it does not fit the nineteenth-

century national sentiments of the General? Despite a snail's pace, but because of French insistence, the integrated agricultural marketing system is beginning to operate for certain commodities, even though no single interest group or government seems to be completely happy with it. The harmonization of turn-over taxes is making slow progress under the active mediation of the EEC Commission. The first regulations concerning a harmonized social security system have come into operation. Europe has its first modest common regulation governing competition, even though the appreciably different approaches of the Common Market and the Coal and Steel treaties are creating confusion in this realm. The relative inflexibility of the Coal and Steel treaty, even though this was supposed to conduce to stronger supranational powers, also clashes with the more permissive approach of the Common Market treaty in the fields of transport policy, aid to redundant industries and national subsidies, with the result that very little has been done in these areas. Lack of success in agreeing to a common energy policy is partially attributable to the same cause, even though the governments of France and Italy also have here shown that so far they are quite unwilling to subordinate the national to the European interest. Another reason for lack of success lies in the adamant opposition between private and public interests identified with coal and oil, respectively, in each nation. In these fields, then, the spill-over has turned into a trickle.

But this does not exhaust the picture. The Court of the Communities has recently pronounced its equivalent of Marbury v. Madison in the *Van Gend* Case, laying down clearly the supremacy of Community law and holding that it applies directly to the individual citizen. Several European governments were found guilty of violating portions of the Treaty of Rome; in all cases they faithfully carried out the court's rulings. The Netherlands, in exchange for accepting the Community's association agreement with eighteen African states (an agreement which conduces primarily to the benefit of France), extracted a promise that in the future single vetoes could not validly hold 'up the association of additional outside countries. Despite the exclusion of Britain numerous countries still feel sufficiently attracted to or threatened by the Community to demand the opening of negotiations for some form of economic association with it. All these manifestations imply a continuation of the spill-over process despite the preferences of the most active opponents of supranational integration. . . .

To what extent is the future of Europe determined by this version

of the past? It seems to me incontestable that the future is determined in the sense that the supremacy of welfare-dominated policies
is assured. If supranational institutions already charged with further
penetrating this field are firmly anchored in this supremacy, they will
survive and flourish. Determined is the role of the technocrat, the
technical expert whose statistics and negotiations fashion welfare
policies, whether this technocrat is on the payroll of a powerful
interest group, a national government or a supranational executive.
Determined is the citizen's distrust of simplistic nationalist slogans,
the realization of which would involve him in sacrificing his peace or
his standard of living. Determined, therefore, is indifference to militarism, adventurism and heroics. If by the term "americanization"
we merely mean the progressive *embourgeoisement* of tastes and behavior patterns which goes along with industrial society in the West
as well as in the East, then the americanization of the New Europe
is equally determined.

What is far from determined by history, however, is the extent of
the region so ruled, the degree of supranationality the rule will imply,
and the region's relationship with the rest of the western industrialized world. . . .

RAYMOND ARON

Old Nations, New Europe

Raymond Aron (born 1905), French journalist and University professor, has written several works in international relations, among which his Peace and War Among Nations *(1962) contributes most originally to the theory of historical sociology. His articles, which are syndicated throughout Europe, appear regularly in* Figaro *of which he has been a staff member since 1947. M. Aron, a ranking European political and economic commentator, is currently Professor at the Institute d'Etudes Politiques and in the Faculty of Arts at the University of Paris (Sorbonne).*

IN WHAT SENSE . . . is it possible to speak of Europe in the singular, as if it constituted a unit? First and foremost, it is the view of others that transforms a diversity into a whole. It is the non-Europeans or better yet the ex-Europeans—that is, the majority of Americans—who call Europe the Old Continent and who see in it specific traits that make it different from the New World. The initial impulse for the European unification movement came from Stalin, who threatened us all, and from Marshall, who made close cooperation between European nations the condition of his plan.

The nations of Europe also form a community in itself (*an sich*) in the sense that they have enough traditions and values in common to merit recognition as one and the same historical civilization (or culture in the sense of that word as used by Spengler and Toynbee); yet this sort of unity already existed yesterday and it has nothing in common with the political unity aspired to by those who are called "Europeans." . . .

Finally, in order to exist as such and not only as a common culture in the eyes of others, Europe must become either an economic unit or a political unit, or better still, both economically and politically

From Raymond Aron, "Old Nations, New Europe," *Daedalus* (Winter, 1964). Reprinted by permission of the American Academy of Arts and Sciences.

unified at the same time. In short, there will not be a historical revolution properly speaking, except to the extent that nation-states,
which seemed to nineteenth-century historians the supreme form of
political organization, are in the process of melting into a larger
whole, into a superior form.

The polls . . . suggest that the citizens of the Six will be ready to
abandon sovereignty (since the majority of them accept the notion
of a common foreign policy). But this consent signifies almost nothing.
The man in the street has a very dim idea of what a common diplomacy could be. Such decisions are neither taken by the majority,
nor do they carry out the preferences of the majority; they are taken
by the ruling minorities. Furthermore, the same Dutch who subscribe
to a common foreign policy would willingly substitute Great Britain
for France in the Common Market. . . .

Some Common Market nations feel closer to certain nations outside
of the European Community than they do to other members of it.
The Six are only one part of Europe considered geographically and
culturally. Can the Six form a confederation? Do they wish to? How
does the rest of Europe stand in relation to the community?

Following the success of the Coal and Steel Pool and the defeat
of the European army, the European party, which had followed the
lead of Jean Monnet, decided to turn back to economics. The Treaty
of Rome was signed and the first steps toward a customs union were
successfully taken. . . .

Enthusiasts for the Common Market used to think and willingly
said that political unity—a single government—would result spontaneously and inevitably from economic unity. Others, like M.
Monnet, were not aiming for the constitution of a European state,
a great power comparable to the other superpowers. For them the
Coal and Steel Pool and the Treaty of Rome were neither ends in
themselves nor means to predetermined ends. They were the means
for a *planned institutional transformation.* They were creating institutions which would transform reality and which were themselves
destined to change as reality changes.

Both conceptions have recently received a severe blow. In M.
Monnet's eyes, Great Britain's request to join the Common Market
was the normal result of the latter's success. Experience had bril-
liantly proved the benefits of the Common Market; Great Britain,
skeptical of ideas as usual, would pay attention to facts and learn
the lesson. Up to the last moment M. Monnet refused to believe that

the Brussels negotiations would fail. Probably even today the setback appears to him temporary, opposed to the inevitable nature of things.

As for those, more Marxist than they realize, who do not doubt that there is an inevitably smooth progression from economic unity to political unity, they are doubly mistaken. The Treaty of Rome, apart from the dismantling of customs barriers, is primarily a catalogue of tasks and intentions. Everything remains to be done in regard to harmonizing legislation and common agricultural policy; it can be done only if the various governments wish to reach agreement. In other words, the *text does not create an automatic unification.* It urges the governments to reach an agreement *to the extent that they refuse, on principle, to resign themselves to disagreement.* In the second place, even if they form a single economic unity, the six nations are not obliged to have one identical foreign policy. It is pure fantasy to imagine that the governments of Bonn and Paris will necessarily take the same attitude toward East Germany on the day that goods, capital and men circulate freely between France and West Germany.

The controversy between the partisans of a Europe of States and an integrated Europe has rarely reached the heart of the matter. To give—on paper—such and such so-called supranational powers to the High Authority or to the European Commission is not sufficient to place these agencies in a position to resolve differences or to impose decisions on the national governments. In this sense, the partisans of a Europe of States are not wrong in casting doubt on the importance of the particular structure of institutions; and it is even less true that regular meetings of government leaders or ministers should, in the long run, create the unity to which they claim to aspire. The real question is different and it is much more basic: Do the old nations wish to abdicate in favor of the young Europe—and can they? Do Frenchmen, Germans and Italians wish to be Europeans in the sense that citizens of Geneva, Zurich or Berne are Swiss citizens? I have never been convinced that the answer to this question is in the affirmative. And the advent of Gaullism in France makes such an answer still more uncertain. . . .

In one sense General de Gaulle's responsibility for the present crisis cannot be questioned. He himself proclaims it aloud. But sooner or later Europeans would have come, in one way or another, to ask those questions of principle whose resolution they had been leaving to time and experience. What kind of Europe do they wish? Do they wish a federated Europe, capable of defending itself and limited to states willing to sacrifice their sovereignty? Do they wish a Europe which will be a great power dealing with the Soviet Union and the United States as an equal? Do they wish an enlarged Europe, including Great Britain, Denmark and Norway, which will leave the main responsibility for defense to the United States? In short, are the old nations, theoretically not opposed to a common diplomacy, capable of having one? In other words, do they have the same image of the world, of their goals and their interests? The present crisis obliges us to answer this question in the negative.

The German Federal Republic is dependent on the United States for its security, and it is therefore especially anxious to assure the maintenance of American troops in Europe and to do nothing that would provoke American leaders into a policy of disengagement. Incapable of achieving a national deterrent force, West Germany still hopes to participate in nuclear strategy, and for this reason it favors military integration in NATO. De Gaulle's France harbors a national ambition to possess its own deterrent force and is opposed to all forms of military integration. It does not, for the moment, reject the Atlantic Alliance, but it claims to see in it only a provisional organization, useful until the day when the Soviet Union, having reverted to the Old Russia, will favor the reconciliation of the two halves of the Old Continent. The supranational institutions recommended by M. Monnet's party can contribute to the realization of an integrated economy, but they cannot give to the various nations the unity of vision and goals which a common diplomacy requires. . . .

To simplify the situation, it could be said that there are four pairs of alternatives: 1) Europe in the narrow sense (the Six) or a greater Europe (with Great Britain and the Scandinavian nations); 2) an integrated Europe or a Europe of States; 3) an autonomous (independent) Europe or an Atlantic Europe; 4) a Europe possessing a nuclear force or a Europe militarily integrated in an Atlantic alliance in which the United States retains a thermonuclear monopoly. General de Gaulle would choose the first in each of these pairs of alternatives except the second, a fact which gives rise to doubt about his real intentions. Probably he is following a basically French policy, without forgetting that on the day when the Americans leave Europe or when the Soviet Union has become a bourgeois state, France, with its own deterrent force, will play a decisive role in the reorganization of western Europe and in the reconciliation of the two halves of the Old Continent. France's partners would accept a small Europe if it were at least integrated, but they refuse the combination of the small Europe with a Europe of States. Their position is: If Europe is not to be integrated, then it should at least be a larger unit.[1]

With regard to the first pair of alternatives, France's partners in the Six would refuse on either-or choice and declare themselves for an autonomous Europe within the Atlantic Alliance. Finally, on the question of defense, up to now only the British and the Germans seem interested in it. The British hesitate between the Gaullist position of a strictly national force—until recently their own position—and acceptance of a unified Atlantic deterrent force. The Germans do not challenge the American strategic monopoly.

Is this confusion temporary? I am not sure. The creation of a superior political unity, embracing old nations weighed down by history like Great Britain, Germany or France, demands a real political will—unless it is to be a sort of abdication. But a political will is inseparable from a will to be independent, even if it is not equivalent to a will to power. Many of the Brussels Eurocrats are conscious of this fact and see the constitution of a European state, capable of taking a stand and thus of defending itself, as the inevitable final outcome of their efforts. Such a Europe would not consequently be a third force; it would remain tied to the United States, but as a single unit, whereas today, within the alliance, the United States can easily impose its will on the plurality of states, small or middle-sized, whose connections with each other are less close than their subservient relations with the Big Brother across the Atlantic. Such a will to create a politically and militarily united Europe seems to me to be almost nonexistent in the Scandinavian countries (which have always been more Atlantic than European), and feeble in Italy, Holland and Belgium. . . .

Events may invalidate such an analysis. . . . [B]ut after all, nearly twenty years after the end of World War II and thirteen years after the start of the Schuman Plan, it is legitimate to draw up a balance sheet, however provisory.

1. The old nations, which were ruining themselves and imperiling a common civilization, have overcome their memories and their resentments. They have learned to live together and to live in peace. Economic development and its concomitant well-being have facilitated this reconciliation. This gain can be considered solid without undue optimism.

---

[1] An integrated Europe gives better safeguards to the small states than a Europe composed of sovereign states. Belgium and the Netherlands are slightly afraid of a Franco-German common policy whose weight would be decisive in the councils of the Six.

2. On the economic plane, cooperation within the Common Market and sometimes outside it has become the rule. . . . The question of whether or not Britain will finally join the Common Market has probably less economic importance than either its advocates or its adversaries are inclined to think at present. The common external tariff is not and will not be raised to a point which will constitute a serious obstacle to trade. The dichotomy, repeatedly emphasized in the British and American press, between an "inward-looking" and an "outward-looking" community, seems to me to belong to the sphere of polemic and propaganda. . . .

3. It must be admitted that the exclusion of Great Britain, and especially the way in which General de Gaulle did it, has shaken both the European Community and the Atlantic Alliance, but it is useful on this point not to lose a sense of proportion and to resist the pressures of the moment. If the Brussels negotiations had failed because of technical difficulties, nobody would have thought it a catastrophe for the Common Market to be limited to the Six and for the three groups (the European Community, the small free trade zone and the British Commonwealth, the United States) to continue within the Atlantic Alliance. . . .

Will the old nations, with their centuries-old concern for national sovereignty, survive? Is the passion with which the public supports national athletic teams a symbol of a nationalism which raises still another insurmountable obstacle to block federation? Yes and no. I believe that consciousness of the nation remains infinitely stronger than a sense of Europe. I do not perceive any European nationalism beyond an aspiration to a degree of autonomy in relation to the United States and, especially, to the rejection of the bloody quarrels of the past. Will this reasonable desire be enough to give birth to a European federation? In terms of the next twenty years, I do not think so, and I am not even sure it would be desirable, because on this point General de Gaulle seems to me absolutely right: to exist as a political unit, Europe would have to acquire the capacity to defend itself, or at least to acquire a relative autonomy in the Atlantic Alliance. Without this political will, Europe will have to settle for continued economic growth, with the Common Market tightening bonds with Great Britain and the other European nations in one way or another. Will the situation arouse the European nations to a massive effort to acquire a deterrent force in the next twenty years? What will be the relations among China, Russia and the United States?

Nobody seems to me to be in a position to answer these questions, yet it is these answers that will determine the ultimate significance of the European undertaking. The old nations still live in the hearts of men, and love of the European nation is not yet born—assuming that it ever will be. But the federation of the Old Continent is held in check less by the survival of nationalism, large or small, than by another cause, simpler and often unrecognized: the present mixture of cooperation and integration in Europe and within the Atlantic Alliance is sufficient to assure the achievement of prosperity and security. It is not sufficient to create a European state. Rather, one must ask: What would be the object of a European state? To have a sense of vocation, Europe would have to discover a goal. What could this common goal be? A will to push Soviet Communism out of eastern Europe? But if this Soviet retreat is to be peaceful, is a European bloc something to be hoped for or something to be feared? A will to become a great power? But, in the nuclear world, do we want one more superpower?

A EUROPE OF STATES OR
A SUPRANATIONAL EUROPE?

CHARLES DE GAULLE

A Europe of States

The following selections, from three of President de Gaulle's press conferences, covering a period from 1960 to 1965, present his views of what he calls "the realities of Europe."

Third Press Conference, September 5, 1960

... TO BUILD EUROPE, that is to say, to unite it, is evidently something essential. It is trite to ask why this great center of civilization, of strength, of reason, of prosperity is being smothered by its own ashes. All that is necessary, in such a domain, is to proceed, not by following our dreams, but according to realities.

Now, what are the realities of Europe? What are the pillars on which it can be built? The States are, in truth, certainly very different from one another, each of which has its own spirit, its own history, its own language, its own misfortunes, glories and ambitions; but these States are the only entities that have the right to order and the authority to act. To imagine that something can be built that would be effective for action and that would be approved by the peoples outside and above the States—this is a dream.

Of course it is true that, while waiting to come to grips with Europe's problem and tackle it as a whole, it has been possible to

The first two selections are excerpted from *Major Addresses, Statements and Press Conferences of General Charles de Gaulle (May 19, 1958-January 31, 1964)*, published by Press and Information Division, French Embassy, New York. The last selection is from "The Atlantic Alliance: Allied Comment," prepared by the Subcommittee on National Security and International Operations of the Committee on Government Operations, U. S. Senate (89th Congress, 2nd Session), United States Government Printing Office, 1966.

institute certain organs that are more or less extranational. These organs have their technical value, but they do not have, they cannot have authority and, consequently, political effectiveness. As long as nothing serious happens, they function without much difficulty, but as soon as a tragic situation appears, a major problem to be solved, it can then be seen that one "High Authority" or another has no authority over the various national categories and that only the States have it. . . .

Once again, it is quite natural that the States of Europe have at their disposal specialized organs for the problems that they have in common, in order to help formulate and, if need be, follow up their decisions; but the right to take these decisions is theirs alone. To ensure regular cooperation between the States of Western Europe is what France considers as desirable, possible and practical in the political, economic, and cultural domains and in that of defense.

This requires organized, regular consultation between responsible Governments, and then the work of specialized organs in each of the common domains which are subordinate to the Governments. This requires periodic deliberations by an assembly formed of delegates from the national parliaments, and in my opinion, this will have to require, as soon as possible, a formal European referendum so as to give this launching of Europe the character of popular support and initiative that is indispensable.

As it happens the States of Europe have at present between them, in common, great means of action and also, very great problems. As it happens their former enmities are being reduced to minor proportions. In short, as it happens, the opportunity is at hand. Certainly, if this course is taken, if one can hope that we shall embark on it, ties will be increased and habits will take shape. Then, as time does its work, little by little, it is possible that new steps will be taken toward European unity. . . .

Sixth Press Conference, May 15, 1962
. . . I would like incidentally . . . to point out to you . . . that I have never personally, in any of my statements, spoken of a "Europe of nations," although it is always being claimed that I have done so. It is not, of course, that I am repudiating my own; quite the contrary, I am more attached to France than ever, and I do not believe that Europe can have any living reality if it does not include France and her Frenchmen, Germany and its Germans, Italy and its Italians, and so forth. Dante, Goethe, Chateaubriand belong to all Europe

to the very extent that they were respectively and eminently Italian, German and French. They would not have served Europe very well if they had been stateless, or if they had thought and written in some kind of integrated Esperanto or Volapük.

But it is true that the nation is a human and sentimental element, whereas Europe can be built on the basis of active, authoritative and responsible elements. What elements? The States, of course; for, in this respect, it is only the States that are valid, legitimate and capable of achievement. I have already said, and I repeat, that at the present time there cannot be any other Europe than a Europe of States, apart, of course, from myths, stories and parades. What is happening with regard to the Economic Community proves this every day, for it is the States, and only the States, that created this Economic Community, that furnished it with funds, that provided it with staff members; and it is the States that give it reality and efficiency, all the more so as it is impossible to take any far-reaching economic measure without committing a political action.

It is a political action, when tariffs are dealt with in common, when coal-mining areas are converted, when wages and social welfare funds are made the same in the six States, when each State allows workers from the five other States to settle on its territory, when decrees are consequently taken and when Parliament is asked to vote necessary laws, funds and sanctions. It is a political action when agriculture is included in the Common Market, and it is the six States, and they alone, that succeeded in doing so last January by means of their political bodies. It is a political action when the association of Greece or of the African States or of the Malagasy Republic is being dealt with. It is a political action when one negotiates with Great Britain on the request that it has made to enter the Common Market. It is again a political action when the applications of other States for participation or association are considered. It is still a political action when one comes to consider the requests that the United States announces that it will make with regard to its economic relations with the Community.

In fact, the economic development of Europe cannot be assured without its political union. . . .

I should like to speak more particularly about the objection to integration. The objection is presented to us with the words, "Let us merge the six States into a supranational entity; this way, things will be quite simple and practical." But such an entity cannot be found without there being in Europe today a federator with sufficient power, authority and skill. That is why one falls back on a type of hybrid, in which the six States would undertake to comply with what will be decided upon by a certain majority. At the same time, although there are already six national Parliaments, plus the European Parliament, plus the Consultative Assembly of the Council of Europe . . . we must, it seems, elect yet another parliament, a so-called European one—which would lay down the law for the six States.

These are ideas that may, perhaps, beguile certain minds, but I certainly do not see how they could be carried out in practice, even if there were six signatures on the dotted line. Is there a France, a Germany, an Italy, a Holland, a Belgium, a Luxembourg, that would be ready—in a matter that is important for them from the national or the international point of view—to do something that they would consider bad because this would be dictated to them by others? Would the French people, the German people, the Italian people, the Dutch people, the Belgian people, or the Luxembourg people dream of submitting to laws voted by foreign deputies if these laws were to run contrary to their own deep-seated will? This is not so; there is no way, at the present time, for a foreign majority to be able to constrain recalcitrant nations. It is true that, in this "integrated" Europe, as they say, there would perhaps be no policy at all. This would simplify things a great deal. Indeed, once there would be no France and no Europe, once there would be no policy—since no one policy could be imposed on each of the six States—one would refrain from making any policies at all. But then, perhaps, this world would follow the lead of some outsider who did have a policy. There would perhaps be a federator, but the federator would not be European. And it would not be an integrated Europe, it would be something quite different, much broader and much more extensive with, I repeat, a federator. . . .

You see, when one's mind dwells on matters of great import, it is pleasant to dream of the marvelous lamp that Aladdin had only to rub in order to soar above the real. But there is no magic formula that will make it possible to build something as difficult as a united Europe. Thus, let us place reality at the basis of the edifice and, when we shall have completed the work, this will be the time for us to lull ourselves to sleep with the tales of "The Thousand and One Nights."

Twelfth Press Conference, September 9, 1965

. . . The three treaties, which respectively set up the E.C.S.C., Euratom and the Common Market, were concluded before France's recovery in 1958. . . . [E]ach of the three treaties instituted an appearance of an executive in the form of a commission independent from the States—although its members were appointed and remunerated by them—and an appearance of a legislature in the form of an Assembly bringing together members of the various parliaments, yet without their electors having given them any mandate that was not national. This claim held by a technocracy, for the most part foreign, destined to infringe upon France's democracy in settling problems that dictate the very existence of our country, obviously could not suit our purposes once we were determined to take our destiny into our own hands.

Who can ignore that the idea of grouping the States of Western Europe together from the economic and, I might add, political standpoints has long been ours? As far as the economy is concerned, we indeed think it is true that the organized adjustment of the respective activities of the countries located on both sides of the Rhine and the Alps corresponds to the fact that they are close neighbors; that, from the standpoint of production, they are both similar and complementary; and that it is in keeping with the conditions of our times to create entities more vast than each of the European States. In addition, France, who is making great strides forward and whose currency has become one of the world's strongest, has every reason to cast off her former protectionism and to open herself progressively to competition. That is why, for seven years, we have very actively helped to build the Economic Community. . . . But what we wanted yesterday and what we want today is a community that is fair and reasonable.

Fair: that means that agricultural products, allowing for their own particular conditions, should be included in the Common Market concurrently with industrial goods. Reasonable: that means that nothing which is important at present in the organization, and later in the operation of the Common Market of the Six, should be decided and, even more, applied, except by the responsible public authorities in the six States, that is, the Governments controlled by the Parliaments.

Now, we know . . . that there is a different concept of a European federation in which, according to the dreams of those who conceived it, the countries would lose their national personalities, and in which, furthermore, for want of a federator—such as, in the West, Caesar and his successors, Charlemagne, Otto I, Charles V, Napoleon and Hitler tried to be, each in his fashion, and such as, in the East, Stalin tried to be—would be ruled by some technocratic, stateless and irresponsible Areopagus. We know also that France is opposing this project, which contradicts all reality, with a plan for organized cooperation among the States, evolving, doubtless, toward a confederation. This plan alone seems to France to be consistent with what the nations of our continent actually are. It alone could one day make possible the adherence of countries such as Britain or Spain which, like ours, could in no way accept the loss of their sovereignty. It alone would make the future entente of all of Europe conceivable. . . .

We are in a century that has reached the two-thirds mark in its course, no more. However, since the turn of the century, the world has undergone changes unprecedented in their pace and their scope. Everything leads one to think that the trend is going to continue. For a whole series of facts of far-reaching significance is in the making to reshape the world.

In this series of facts, there is: the accession to sovereignty of a large number of States that have been created or restored since the war and, simultaneously, the unfolding of their reciprocal quarrels; the preponderant power acquired by two countries, America and Russia, which induces them to compete with each other and to align under their respective hegemonies the peoples within their reach; the extremely profound gestation that is taking place in enormous China and that destines her for a leading role in the world; the existence and increase in nuclear weapons capable of destroying great nations suddenly and utterly; finally and above all, the general driving force for progress that the opportunities of the modern industrial age are opening up in each region of the earth. In short, the world, in full evolution, is filled both with almost infinite hopes and gigantic dangers.

Confronted with this situation, what can France's role be? But first, must France have a role? There is no lack of people, as you know, who think not. According to them, we—no longer being able to act by ourselves politically, economically, technically and militarily— should henceforth allow ourselves to be led by others. Moreover, the ideologies are there to cover up this renouncement. Thus some in our country, employing the screen of the International, would like to submit us to Moscow's obedience. Others, invoking either arbitrary theories or the convenience of interests, profess that our country should efface its personality in international organizations made in such a way that the United States can exercise in them, from within or without, a preponderant action with which, by definition, we have only to conform. It is in this way that those people conceive of our participation in the United Nations or NATO and desire that we see ourselves dissolved in a federation called "European" which would actually be "Atlantic." . . .

Above all, it is a question of keeping ourselves free of any vassalage. It is true that, in many areas, we have the best reasons for associating with others. But on condition of retaining our self-determination. Thus, so long as the solidarity of the Western peoples appears to us neccessary for the eventual defense of Europe, our country will remain the ally of her allies but, upon the expiration of the commitments formerly taken—that is, in 1969 by the latest—the subordination known as "integration" which is provided for by NATO and which hands our fate over to foreign authority shall cease, as far as we are concerned. Thus, while working to unite the States on both sides of the Rhine and the Alps, from the economic, political, cultural and strategic viewpoints, we are making sure that this organization does not deprive us of our free will. . . .

HANS NORD

A Supranational European Community

Hans Nord, an international civil servant, has served as President of the European Movement in the Netherlands (1958–61), Chairman of the Netherlands Atlantic Committee (1954–61), and Secretary-General of the European Parliamentary Assembly (1961–present). In addition to the article from which this excerpt was taken, his publications include "Problems of International Government" (1948), "International and Supra-National Cooperation" (1952), and "NATO" (1961).

CAN EUROPEAN INTEGRATION be effected by voluntary co-operation between national governments, or do we need independent European institutions with authority of their own? In other words, is the framework we seek to be intergovernmental or supranational?

. . . [I]t has become fashionable not to mention the word *supranational*. Does this mean that the concept of a European community, with common institutions endowed with powers of their own within their designated fields, has to be given up? I do not think so. A real alternative has not been given and the basic facts and requirements of our situation have not changed.

If one accepts the aims of integration as I have indicated them, one cannot escape the conclusion that the supranational community is the only possible political framework for European integration.

In any permanent alliance or community of states, the problem of power is paramount. . . .

No society can function effectively without the exercise of authority. Without such authority European integration cannot be brought about. No measure of integration achieved can be safeguarded without it. The common European interest which integra-

From Hans Nord, "In Search of a Political Framework for an Integrated Europe," in *European Integration*, edited by C. Grove Haines (Baltimore, 1957), pp. 217, 219–224. Reprinted by permission of The Johns Hopkins Press.

tion seeks to create and serve is not a simple sum of the various interests of the member states. It will and must exist on its own level and in its own right. The joint exercise of sovereignty which European integration implies must, therefore, rest with organs possessing the power to discharge their task. And, at the same time, these bodies must be subject to a public opinion functioning in the European community as a whole. . . .

It would be futile to attempt to draw a precise blueprint for a European political structure at the present stage. The making of Europe resembles the work of the gardener rather than that of the engineer. The European Community, which must embody unity while respecting, and even honoring, diversity, will have to grow. But its growth will depend primarily on the nature of the seed that has been planted. This simple truth is too often forgotten. The illusion persists that institutions without powers will somehow automatically evolve into institutions with powers. Although it would be useless to indulge in the drafting of a full-blown European constitution, the experience of recent years and the requirements of European integration itself make it possible and highly necessary to define more clearly and systematically the principles according to which a supranational European community should be brought into being. There are a number of points which, in this connection, are essential. First, we should not try to copy forms evolved, however successfully, in other parts of the world. . . . We shall have to find and develop our own forms of association and however much we may be inspired by what others achieved before us, we must remember that twentieth-century Europe presents problems for which new solutions, suitable to our own surroundings and political traditions, will have to be worked out.

This brings me to my second point, the concept of supranationality itself. We are living in the age of nationalism. The identification of the idea of the state with that of the nation has become, especially in Europe, almost complete. The nation has conquered the state and become its sovereign master and jealous guard. The concept of a supranational community—or, in other words, of a multinational state—therefore implies a fundamental re-thinking of political and constitutional theory in Europe. It means that the idea of the state itself is questioned.

To many people in Europe, accustomed as they are to identifying state and nation, and to regarding the unitary nation-state as the only possible one, because it is the only one they know, a united

Europe means a unitary European state. A great deal of resistance to European integration stems from this fallacy. It cannot be repeated too often that the European Community is something quite different from the new Leviathan some people seem to fear. But, at the same time, it should be stressed that the European Community cannot be built solely with the existing national states as basic units. This danger is very real. It must be averted if European integration is to succeed.

Let us imagine for a moment what would happen if we chose the easy way and, using the present European pattern as a basis, completed our political framework by giving authority and powers of decision to bodies composed of representatives of the various national sovereignties. Such bodies would be supranational in the sense that their decisions would be binding. In order to reach these decisions, votes would have to be taken by majority, simple or qualified as the case might be. Every question would inevitably become more, not less, national. For instance, Benelux would be beaten by France, Germany, and Italy, or France would be outvoted by a combination of Germany and Benelux, with Italy abstaining. Many combinations are possible. It is clear that such a framework would only irritate and at the same time strengthen political nationalism in Europe. The European Community would become a battlefield for national interests, seeking majority positions within the organs of the community. Such a construction would be both a mockery and a tragedy. Also, it would not be able to withstand for long the terrible strain of conflicting national interests, for these, instead of being sublimated on a higher European level, would be, as it were, institutionalized and thereby artificially kept alive.

This, then, is what our supranational community should not become. No superstate, no authority giving orders to member governments and acting on and through them. The only sane framework for an integrated Europe is that which recognizes that the European and the national interests are both valid and have to be organized separately. There can be no subordination of national governments to a European government. They are both independent within their designated fields. In other words, the European Community cannot be built on the existing member nations alone—it must rest on a European citizenry. That is the only way to serve the interests of Europe and also that of its nations and their peoples. Every European must know that he is a citizen of his nation and also of the

European Community. Only in that way can the conflict between nationalism and European integration be resolved. This is the new idea of the state which will have to be brought home to Europeans.

My third point is a logical corollary from what has preceded. It concerns the democratic control of the process of integration and of the European Community which will emerge from it.

The rise of democracy, of government by consent, has been a long process requiring constant effort and vigilance. In Europe, democracy is now being threatened not only by the forces of totalitarianism but also by the very insufficiency of the national states to perform the functions which are theirs. We can no longer afford to determine our national policies independently, or even at the expense of our neighbors. . . .

If one accepts the concept of supranationality as the only valid one for European integration, the necessity for a common European parliament is obvious. It is obvious for three reasons: first, because integration cannot be achieved without the consent of the peoples expressing themselves through their representatives; second, because a European executive authority needs the complementary partner which only a parliamentary body can provide; and third, because integration without democratic control would lead to the progressive decay of democracy in Europe.

One cannot speak of a European parliament without broaching the question of European elections. This is a much debated matter, and many arguments are put forward on both sides. What should our decision be?

. . . To present-day Europeans, a parliament with authority is a parliament which has been directly elected. That is a reality which we cannot afford to overlook.

It is often said that our people are not ripe for European elections because European problems are too far removed from their daily lives. There is certainly truth in this. But do we honestly believe that our national electorates are so well versed in the problems with which their national representatives have to deal? The argument about ripeness is a two-edged sword.

A great deal depends, of course, on the electoral system that would be used. It is natural to assume that, in the beginning, a system would be selected which would change very little the existing national political parties presenting their own "European" candidates to a national electorate. . . . However, it may be regarded as certain that the first European elections would not produce any startling or revolutionary change. But they would open up new possibilities for the future. European problems are going to present new issues which no longer correspond to existing party political labels or to national points of view.

Gradually, therefore, European programs will come into being and a fresh breeze will blow through the political life of our Continent. Something resembling European parties, bound together by common European objectives, will play its part in reinforcing popular loyalty to the new community and in creating a new interest in public affairs.

The fourth point concerns the protection of our free way of life and our fundamental liberties. Modern history has seen the rise of the criminal state. It has been painfully brought home to us that the protection of our liberties transcends national boundaries and that common measures are indispensable to safeguard our freedom. In Europe, the Convention of Human Rights, with its Human Rights Commission and its Court, represents an important step in this direction. . . .

The European Community must be so constructed that the fundamental liberties of its citizens can be effectively protected and preserved. Not only member states as such, but also individuals and groups of individuals, must be able to appeal when human rights are alleged to have been violated. I stress the importance of this aspect of the European Community. For it may become of the greatest value in dealing with those countries in Europe which at present cannot participate in our joint efforts.

My last point deals with the tension which will inevitably exist between the nations of Europe and the European Community. In the concept of two independent spheres of government, this tension should not be unbearable. It may even act for the common good. But it is essential that the rights of our national communities, however small, be respected. Uniformity is the mortal enemy of European civilization. Tolerance and love of diversity should be our guiding virtues. As our friends from Luxembourg have often put it: "Wir wollen bleiben was wir sind."[1]

In the European Community all peoples will be in a minority. Our political framework should be based upon this fact. A balance must be found between national and European rights, duties, and interests. Without entering into details, it can be said that both the executive and the parliamentary bodies of the community must

[1] "We will remain what we are." [Editor's note.]

reflect this dual character. Some form of bicameral system will be indispensable.

These, then, are five principles which should be regarded as basic for a real and organic European Community.

J. B. DUROSELLE

General de Gaulle's Europe and Jean Monnet's Europe

J. B. Duroselle is Director of the Centre d'Etudes des Relations Internationales in Paris and Professor of International Relations in the Faculté des Lettres at the University of Paris. Among other works he has written The Idea of Europe In History (*Paris, 1965*).

I HOPE I SHALL BE EXCUSED for having chosen a topic which is related to the names of two Frenchmen; my justification is that both these men, General de Gaulle and Jean Monnet, have played, and are playing, an important part in European international relations. They are as different as two men can be; what they have in common is the influence which they exert. Perhaps behind their differences, in spite of the fact that each of them considers the other's concepts and actions as dangerous, there remains a secret mutual esteem and admiration. But the ways in which they conceive of the future of Europe are contradictory, and it is that contradiction which I would like to analyse. . . .

General de Gaulle's Europe

In attempting to define General de Gaulle's Europe, I would stress four points. It is a Europe of independent States, with no supranational authority; a Europe independent of the United States; a Europe in which the dominant Power in foreign policy would be France; and a Europe open to the East.

A EUROPE OF INDEPENDENT STATES WITH NO SUPRANATIONAL AUTHORITY

This idea is well known; but where does it come from? Probably from a highly original concept of the State. In General de Gaulle's view it is very difficult to become a real State. If I may be permitted

From J. B. Duroselle, "General de Gaulle's Europe and Jean Monnet's Europe," *The World Today*, Vol. 22, No. 1 (January, 1966). Reprinted by permission of The Royal Institute of International Affairs and of the author.

to exaggerate a little, I would say that there are, in his opinion, only two States in the full sense of the term, Britain and France: first Britain and second France. Historically, Britain became a modern State before France did; this is a rather disturbing fact, but nothing can be done about it. But France must be ranked as high as Britain. One of the most stimulating hypotheses in the interpretation of General de Gaulle's policy is precisely his admiration for Britain, and his deep conviction that the old Franco-British rivalry for precedence continues. . . .

Other States are, in General de Gaulle's view, far behind these two historical leaders. The United States has a Constitution which goes, as he says, "cahin-caha." Russia (the General hardly ever uses the expression 'the Soviet Union') is poisoned by Communism; but he is convinced that Communism will disappear one day, and is only an episode in her history. Italy and Germany are far from being really united. General de Gaulle never speaks of East Germany; he always says "Prussia and Saxony."

The results of this idea of the supreme value of individual States are twofold. First, the States—the real ones—are bound to survive ideologies; secondly, they cannot be absorbed or merged into something bigger and supranational. It is well known that, as regards purely economic matters, General de Gaulle is in favour of the Common Market; it is also well known that the strong alliance, whether right or wrong, between de Gaulle and Adenauer in 1958 saved the Common Market from being absorbed into the free trade area proposed by Britain. But now that economic matters, because of the progress of the Common Market, are tending more and more to have political connotations, de Gaulle is increasingly cautious. The breakdown of negotiations on agricultural problems on 30 June . . . [1965] is probably due to this fact. The powers of the European Commission, "a technocracy composed of a majority of foreigners," must not be allowed to destroy the individual State's right of self-determination. Majority voting, due to come into effect on 1 January 1966, has to be got rid of by some kind of gentleman's agreement. Whereas Jean Monnet's postulate is that economic integration is good *because it will* necessarily, some day, produce political integration, for de Gaulle, it is good only so long as *it does not* produce political integration.

A EUROPE INDEPENDENT OF THE UNITED STATES
    This is also a well-known aspect of de Gaulle's Europe. He has gradually come to the view that the Brussels Commission is the in-

strument of a U.S.-dominated Europe. One of the many reasons why he rejected Britain's application to enter the Common Market was because after he had met Mr. Macmillan at Rambouillet there occurred the Kennedy-Macmillan meeting at Nassau in which he felt Britain knuckled under to the United States in terms of atomic armaments. Certainly he believes that the Americans, whether consciously or unconsciously, are trying to maintain their "hegemony" over Europe. He sees signs of this attitude in the theory of nuclear non-dissemination, in the influx of American investment into key industries all over Western Europe, in the so-called Kennedy Round, in the Geneva nuclear test ban, etc.

. . . Though de Gaulle is in favour of the Western Alliance, he never hesitates to denounce these tendencies; and this irritates the Americans because they are not conscious of exercising any hegemony or of wanting to do so. On 23 July 1964 de Gaulle said: "Many people . . . have suggested for Europe not an independent policy, which indeed they do not conceive, but an organization unable to have such a policy, connected . . . to an Atlantic, that is to say an American, system, and consequently subordinated to what the U.S. call their leadership." On the contrary, what de Gaulle wants is an independent Europe—a Europe which will be a "third force." On 31 December 1964 he rejected "all the systems which, under cover of 'Supranationality,' or 'Integration,' or 'Atlanticism,' would in fact keep us under a well-known hegemony."

A EUROPE IN WHICH THE DOMINANT POWER IN FOREIGN POLICY WOULD BE FRANCE

General de Gaulle has never spoken openly of such French leadership. The word "supremacy" which appears in the English translation of his memoirs is simply a bad translation of "coopération." But it is clear that what he calls a politically united Europe is a Europe in which the other partners are willing to accept what he thinks is good sense and historical necessity, that is to say, the policy which he proposes of Europe "as a third force." Among the Six, France is the only Power with "world responsibilities." French ideas have to be taken into account, therefore, and he seems to reckon on a Europe in which—as Germany did in Adenauer's latter years—the other partners would follow the general line of French foreign policy. The fact that they do the opposite, that, if they feel the necessity of leadership, they prefer the powerful leader—namely, the United States—to France, does not seem to discourage him. In the end he is sure that good sense will prevail, and the European countries will understand that they should cherish a "European Europe" in which France will definitely be the big brother. (This is one more reason for dismissing the candidacy of Britain, another Power with world responsibilities; it would not be pleasant for France if a second big brother joined the first.)

A EUROPE OPEN TO THE EAST

General de Gaulle has so often said that France will be faithful to the Western Alliance and he has so violently condemned the Communist system that the idea of a shift of alliances is quite absurd. Such an idea has been conceived only in the minds of American newspaper columnists.

But at the same time, he speaks of a "Europe from the Atlantic to the Urals." What does that mean? Very probably, one can assume that he is looking to the long-range future. One day, Europe will be "united"—an association of States in which France will play her appropriate role. Such a Europe is the only Power which will be able to convince the Russians that the reunification of Germany is unavoidable. One day also, Communism will disappear in the U.S.S.R. Meanwhile, it is possible that China, "innumerable and miserable," and the "yellow people" will one day fight against the Soviets, the Europeans, and the Americans. Ultimately they may perhaps conquer Siberia and Soviet Asia. Why should we not imagine that the "Russia" of that time, freed from Bolshevism, would be delighted to join her old partners, as in the times of the European concert following Peter the Great? . . .

Jean Monnet's Europe

. . . I would like to summarize my picture of Jean Monnet's Europe, as I did for that of de Gaulle, by stressing four points. Monnet's Europe is: an anti-nationalist Europe; a Europe based upon concrete institutions; a European Community linked to the United States in a strong partnership; an "open" Europe.

AN ANTI-NATIONALIST EUROPE

Jean Monnet is a "good citizen of his own country," but he hates nationalism, because nationalism is equated in his view with the "spirit of domination." Nationalism is based on inequality, and what needs to be created is the spirit of equality. As he has said: "National sovereignties can oppose one another; nationalism in one country fatally provokes nationalism in the others." While General de Gaulle

exalts French nationalism, Monnet deplores it, not so much because French nationalism could be dangerous in itself, but because
it encourages German nationalism, which is still potentially dangerous.

The consequence is that Monnet's Europe is not founded upon a
new European nationalism which would eliminate local nationalisms,
but is based on something quite new. Many pro-Europeans believe
that a kind of European nationalism has to be developed in public
opinion before Europe can be united. Monnet, who is no sentimental-
ist but a man of action, does not believe that Europe has a prior need
of this new kind of nationalism. After all, Britain, France, and Spain
were united before the "nationalist movement" appeared. And a
European nationalism would eventually bring a united Europe into
opposition against the other big Powers.

A EUROPE BASED UPON CONCRETE INSTITUTIONS

Here I think is Jean Monnet's most original idea, and his greatest
contribution to human history. As he said on 3 October 1965 at a
ceremony at Scy-Chazelles in honour of Robert Schuman: "For a
long time, people spoke of European unity. But words, general ideas,
good intentions were not enough. Concrete action was necessary to
bring that idea to reality. That action was started by the Schuman
Plan." It is a well-known fact that the Schuman Plan originated
from the ideas of Jean Monnet and was then strongly backed by
Robert Schuman, who took the decision and "made the political
choice."

To create an institution is in itself an action; it is also a source of
future creativity. The institution, once it exists, produces concrete
effects; those effects produce something new in the minds of men,
and this is the important point. An institution is immensely more
influential than any amount of propaganda in changing the minds
of men. But what sort of institution? Is there any guiding-line to
determine what has to be done? Yes, indeed. Jean Monnet dis-
covered this from his experience when he worked in London between 1914 and 1918. He had to convince the Allied Governments
that it was better to purchase in common rather than to purchase
separately, to set up a pool of tonnage as a remedy for the shortages
created by the ceaseless German submarine warfare. The normal
reaction of each Government was to act individually. Years of attempts and series of failures were necessary to persuade them to create
such pools, the dominant and very simple idea of which was
"common interest."

Now, in the case of the countries of Europe destroyed and weakened by two wars, the common interest is obvious. National solutions have failed; a common order has to be created. "Only very recently we have started to accept in the relations between our nations what we accept in the relations between men in one country: that force does not prevail, that differences be resolved by common rules, by common institutions." When the Coal and Steel Community was created, the means were established for resolving differences by a common set of rules. Jean Monnet was the first chairman of the High Authority, and he contributed immensely to organizing a common line of action and to developing a common spirit. Here we are far from General de Gaulle's concept of cold-blooded individual States, of international relations from which sentiment has to be eliminated; not of course that Monnet is a sentimental man, but he works to create a "community spirit."

Monnet likes to demonstrate the consistency of his thinking. He certainly had not worked out the concept of "integration" before 1950. But always, from the beginning of his striking career, he has believed in "common interest" fostered by new creative institutions. . . .

Are institutions conceived out of the blue by intelligent and imaginative men? Certainly this does not seem to be the case. An institution has to stem from historical necessity. Monnet is convinced that the regrouping of nations is a historical necessity; that this regrouping is inevitable sooner or later; that there is at each moment in history an optimum size for States; and that France, which now is too small, is faced with the choice between merging into a bigger union or becoming a "superior Spain." He sees another historical necessity in the fact that economic integration will inevitably produce political integration; hence his hostility to de Gaulle when the General tries to break this evolution. Monnet believes that this development will survive de Gaulle's attempts, or alternatively that France will be excluded from this evolution and that another "constellation" of States will be established. He believes that the movement of history will condemn those who work for isolation.

A EUROPEAN COMMUNITY LINKED IN STRONG PARTNERSHIP WITH THE UNITED STATES

Precisely because he is against isolation, Jean Monnet does not conceive of Europe as a "third force" between the United States and the Soviet Union. He believes strongly in Atlantic solidarity, and denies de Gaulle's charges that the Americans have secret aims of hegemony. He is, however, well aware that independence cannot be maintained by European States at the national level.

At the same time, he is not in favour of the expression "Atlantic Community," as long as the United States refuses to surrender to a supranational authority a part of her national sovereignty as the Europeans have to do in the "European Community." Jean Monnet prefers the expression "partnership." It is interesting that President Kennedy, who often used the expression "Atlantic Community"—for instance, in his message on the State of the Union of January 1962—suddenly abandoned this expression and from July 1962 used the other, "Atlantic partnership." This change coincided with one of the many visits Monnet paid to the United States; and this may well be more than a coincidence.

Atlantic partnership means good relations, both politically and economically. But it also has a more concrete aspect. Jean Monnet—and with him his most distinguished disciples, such as Pierre Uri and Etienne Hirsh—are not only against national striking forces, whether French or British, but are also against the creation of a European nuclear force. They consider that it is sufficient to rely on American protection. For this reason Jean Monnet's "Committee for the United States of Europe" has taken a firm stand in favour of a "multilateral nuclear force"—not exactly what the Americans had proposed, but with an increase in the multilateral power of decision.

AN "OPEN EUROPE"

As we have seen, institutions are more important than geography. Therefore, in 1950, Monnet and Schuman preferred a small community consisting of six countries *with* supranational powers rather than a community including Britain but without supranationality; hence the very imperfect Europe of the Six. But this Europe must be open. Monnet welcomed the British application to join and condemned General de Gaulle's decision to reject it. Monnet has never seen in Britain's entry into the Common Market an American "Trojan Horse"; on the contrary, he saw it as a way of escape for the British from the embarrassing position of playing a brilliant "second fiddle." In his view, however, any application for membership must imply the acceptance of the principle of supranationality.

But the European Community is even more open than this. As Monnet says: "Now, the European Community is able to become an equal partner of the United States and so to contribute to the consolidation of the Western world, which is indispensable for the progressive establishment of peaceful coexistence between the West and the Soviet Union." An important difference between de Gaulle and Monnet lies in the fact that de Gaulle believes that Europe *alone*—without the United States—can one day resolve the problem of German reunification, while Monnet thinks that it can be resolved only by a united Europe backed by the United States of America.

Necessity of Choice

The two concepts of Europe which I have outlined above are so contradictory that one cannot think of resolving the dilemma by a compromise. It is essential to choose between them. . . .

But the choice which history will make does not depend on personal preferences or whims. If there were an overwhelming trend of public opinion in favour of an integrated Europe, national Governments would be obliged to take notice of it. But there is nothing of the kind. The majority of Europeans are probably sympathetic to the idea of a United States of Europe, but this sympathy is fragile as soon as it comes up against vested interests; and these tend to become more and more obstructive in proportion as integration develops. . . .

In other words, progress towards integration does not depend exclusively on the disappearance of General de Gaulle from the political scene. The General has applied the brakes by suspending France's participation in the ruling organs of the Common Market on 30 June 1965. But by his ultimatum tactics, he accelerated the creation and development of an agricultural common market. The experts will discuss for a long time to come the question of whether the refusal to admit the United Kingdom on 14 January 1963, whatever may have been its psychological aspects, has injured the integration principle, as Jean Monnet maintains, or has helped it, as André Philip says. Let us imagine that General de Gaulle suddenly disappeared. Must we deduce from this that everything would from then on proceed for the best? That the agricultural problems would be resolved as if by magic? That, with economic integration speeded up in this way, we would arrive painlessly at political integration? I doubt it very much.

One can accept, and I do accept, that what would appear to be Jean Monnet's postulate—namely, that political integration follows necessarily from economic integration—is most likely true. But this certainly does not mean that historical necessity as defined above implies a rapid and easy passage from one to the other. My guess is that if de Gaulle did suddenly disappear we should immediately have other trouble-makers turning up, happy indeed to bring the whole weight of responsibility at the present time down upon the General. Thus, de Gaulle's Europe of a "Concert of Powers," matched by growing economic integration, might simply act as a staging-post, a pause in the building of Europe, a pause which many businessmen, breathless from competition, would accept with relief. After which, if historical necessity does in fact exist, the movement towards integration would be resumed. . . .

The gradual integration of Europe does not depend, in the long run, on the decisions of a few men. But within the time-scale of a decade, Johnson, de Gaulle, and certain others are at liberty to accelerate or slow down its progress.

THE ATLANTIC FRAMEWORK: COMMUNITY OR PARTNERSHIP?

MAURICE ALLAIS

An Integrated Atlantic Community

Maurice Allais, French economist, is Professor of Economic Theory at the Institute of Statistics of the University of Paris and Director of Research at the National Center of Scientific Research. Along with many other works in the area of general economics and economic theory, M. Allais has written "United Europe: Route To Prosperity."

THE PURPOSE OF THIS ESSAY is to try to place the current problems of the Atlantic Community in long-range perspective; to show that it would be to the mutual interest of the Atlantic nations to tighten the political, economic, cultural, and military bonds which unite them, however loose these bonds may appear at present; and to specify what such an orientation implies. . . .

[A] true Atlantic Community appears to be extremely desirable for at least three reasons:

(1) Through its very presence, through the force of attraction it would have, through the very power of its example, it would strongly contribute to the breaking up of the totalitarian ideology which is already in serious difficulties.

(2) Through the strength of its numbers, it would compensate, at least in part, for the disequilibrium of forces resulting from the stronger population expansion in the rest of the world.

Reprinted from *Nato in Quest of Cohesion,* edited by Karl H. Cerny and Henry W. Briefs, and published for The Hoover Institution on War, Revolution, and Peace by Frederick A. Praeger, Inc.

(3) It would constitute progress in itself and be a source of many kinds of progress—social, economic, and cultural; it would represent a new stage in Western civilization, leading to a fuller realization of its possibilities; and it would serve the entire world as an example to follow in order to assure progress and peace.

Obviously there will be disagreement as to what the institutional machinery of a true Atlantic Community ought to be. But whatever the institutions, and allowing a necessary period of transition, a real Atlantic Community would have to be based on: (1) an Atlantic common market, and (2) a basic minimum of common political institutions.

As suggested above, an actual Atlantic Community would imply, on the economic level, a situation in which all artificial obstacles to international movements of goods and factors of production are effectively eliminated. Contrary to an opinion too widely held, the realization of an Atlantic common market is *feasible* and, as far as can be judged, would be *very advantageous* for all its participants. Setting up such a market will inevitably create very serious problems; a complete and immediate opening of frontiers is therefore out of the question. But the problems involved are not beyond mastery. The same problems result from the suppression of trade barriers, tariffs, and quotas in Europe. In the case of an Atlantic market, of course, they would occur on a much larger scale; the advantages for all the participants, however, whatever their level of development, are probably also much greater.

The extensive studies pursued for the past twenty years on achieving a European Common Market show that such problems are technically soluble and that they would be even easier to resolve within the larger framework of an Atlantic Community. Understandably, these studies stress the necessity of a stage-by-stage approach. In this connection, the greater the progress achieved in the first stage of Europe's economic integration—an essential preliminary stage in the total process—the easier will be the implementation of a common Atlantic market.

On the political level, the existence of an effective Atlantic Community would imply extending to the management of all common interests the principles of democratic policy adhered to in each country. In such an Atlantic Community, the participating nations should accept the arrangements made in their common interest and settle differences on the basis of mutually accepted laws and procedures. Such a solution would imply that decisions affecting the common interest would be reached by a weighted, qualified majority among the participating countries.

All of this, obviously, requires the creation of a certain minimum of common political institutions. The discussion of these institutions is outside the scope of the present paper. Suffice it to say that their establishment could only be gradual.

The important point here is that the establishment of a political community, however limited its conception, would mean the transfer of some sovereign rights to a common political authority having *limited but real* powers.

Any confusion that might arise concerning this point should be cleared up at once. In speaking of the transfer of certain sovereign rights belonging to the respective states, it must be understood that this transfer is limited to the *minimum* of rights implied by the effective joint pursuit of the common objectives which have been defined. It must also be understood that *the larger the geographic zone we are considering, the more this transfer can and must be reduced.*

Thus there can be no question of contemplating the transfer to an Atlantic political authority of a body of rights equivalent to the one presently assumed by the American Federal Government, nor even the one which a majority in the "European Six" seem prepared to transfer to the European community. Such a transfer is neither necessary nor desirable. *It is simply a matter of delegating a minimum of rights which, taking into account the experience already acquired, can be considered indispensable for the effective attainment of common objectives. . . .*

The creation of an Atlantic common market, or even of Atlantic-wide trade liberalization, could lead to profound transformations and could in fact be advantageous only if such transformations took place. *Consequently, it would be acceptable only if the participating countries were assured that these transformations were to be, in effect, permanent, that they could not be challenged overnight.*

Economic ties in themselves are fragile. A true common market, or even extensive trade liberalization, are really acceptable only if they are reasonably stable. It follows that economic integration can be accepted and maintained as advantageous only if a certain degree of political integration is carried out at the same time.

Whatever progress has already been made by the European Common Market, *a complete economic integration of Western Europe is conceivable only within the framework of a certain degree of political integration.* Even if all the objectives of the Common Market

Treaty were attained, one would still be quite far from a true common market. . . .

It is not sufficiently realized that progress toward a European Common Market has benefited from a very favorable circumstance, namely, the almost continuous economic expansion that has taken place. A depression could break the established ties very rapidly. Under such conditions there is great danger that the egotistical forces of nationalism would prevail over any regard for European cohesion. . . .

Furthermore, it is doubtful whether one can efficiently prepare a certain degree of political integration by starting in the economic sphere. On the contrary, economic integration reinforces the awareness of the various different national self-interests and, consequently, jeopardizes the development of a real community. In my opinion, *the establishment of at least a minimum of common political institutions must precede, or at least accompany, economic union.* This is an essential condition. The widely held opinion to the contrary is a dangerous illusion.

Seen in this light, one should have no illusion about the possible success of the Kennedy Round in strengthening and extending in a substantial and durable manner the economic ties between Europe and North America. The progress that can be derived from an economic partnership not reinforced by a political partnership will necessarily remain marginal.

I cannot agree with those who maintain that the institutional prerequisite of closer economic interrelations among European countries would not be required in the case of similar relations across the Atlantic. Quite the contrary. In the event of even a relatively moderate policy of trade liberalization, the risks encountered on both sides of the Atlantic would be greater and some of the institutional guarantees which have been considered necessary by the "Six" would be even more indispensable on this broader level.

For the past twenty years the writer of this paper has constantly defended the principle of free trade on national and international levels, advocating a policy of expanding trade on the Atlantic scale. But he would consider as absolutely unrealistic any serious attempts to broaden trade without previously setting up appropriate common economic and political institutions.

The same stricture applies to those who suggest that the functional approach is a valid solution. *The functional approach can be effective only if associated with a vast political conception of unity.*

In and by itself, it can achieve only very limited results. It is unstable and completely unadaptable to the real needs of the peoples of the North Atlantic.

This view does not imply that the general and political approach is easy, or even that it is immediately workable. It simply means that at present the chances of maintaining and strengthening the cohesiveness of the Atlantic alliance are not good, and that it would be very dangerous to think that—for lack of a general and political approach, said to be impossible—traditional policies can provide a valid solution. . . .

If we agree that an effective Atlantic Community would bring positive advantages to the participating nations, it is essential that we see very clearly what its preliminary stages are.

The first necessary step is the transformation, as soon as possible, of the economic Europe of the Six into a political Europe. Without this transformation, one may well doubt whether a true economic Europe is possible, and, *a fortiori,* whether trade liberalization on an Atlantic scale can be accomplished.

The second step is to open the "European Six" to any European nation (particularly to Great Britain) which would accept its fundamental economic and political principles. Only a solidly structured Europe could constitute a desirable and acceptable partner for the United States, and only such a solidly structured Europe could discard the fear of losing its own personality in a closer association with the United States.

The next step would be a substantial effort on the informational and cultural levels. A closer association of Europe and North America would imply a considerable change in the various public opinions.

To state these conditions is to underscore the difficulties. But no human enterprise can succeed without delays, or materialize without some preparation of mind and of the facts. Unless the North Atlantic nations now make the effort to prepare their future with clarity of vision, it is all too probable that they will find themselves disunited and weak at crucial moments. An Atlantic common market and a real Atlantic Community are possible, but not without an effective and permanent political willingness to achieve them by all the participants.

The establishment of a real Atlantic Community and the transfer of certain of the states' sovereign rights to a supranational authority, even on a limited basis, naturally raise numerous objections on which I would like to comment briefly.

An effective Atlantic Community would imply the renunciation of the principle of unlimited national autonomy. But the actual significance of this renunciation is much smaller than appears at first sight.

First of all, the various nations of the West have already renounced a certain part of their national sovereignty. . . . All must take into account the position of their partners in the Atlantic alliance. But this renunciation, however real it may be, is worthless if it is carried on in confusion, disorder, and mutual distrust. Not being related to any real joint action, it is purely negative and serves little purpose. Each of the Western nations suffers the disadvantages of surrendering the principle of unlimited national sovereignty without thereby securing the many advantages which they might reap within an appropriate common political institution.

Secondly, at issue is not so much a surrender of national sovereignty as the delegation by the citizens themselves of a part of their inalienable rights to a superior political authority. In reality, it is simply a transfer, not a surrender. The real objective is not to limit national sovereignty in itself; it is to promote material prosperity and to safeguard fundamental political liberties, peace, and finally, as stressed in the American Constitution, the happiness of the people. The objective is that system of political institutions which is most appropriate to these ends. And if it appears that an Atlantic political community of a certain type might better succeed than our own national institutions, would it not be in the interest of all citizens of the nations involved to support its creation?

In any case, and even within the framework of traditional policies, any treaty, any international obligation is a real limitation of sovereignty the moment one has the positive intention to respect it. Public opinion seems to exaggerate completely the difference between the partial renunciation of national sovereignty implied by respect for treaties and the functioning of an Atlantic Community. Given appropriate safeguards, one wonders if, in all these discussions about a limited renunciation of national sovereignty, we do not attribute more weight to appearances than to realities.

Also, in setting up mutual political arrangements of the type implied by an Atlantic Community, the actual constraints on real independence are far less important than the letter of the agreement might suggest. As the operation of the European Coal and

Steel Community has shown, when the fundamental interests of a participating country were in question, the other countries have always renounced the literal application of the Treaty. Each country knows that if today it fails to take account of its neighbor's difficulties, it may itself be treated similarly in the future. Whatever the situation, the possibility of withdrawal in the course of time is always sufficient to prevent the unreasonable application of the letter of such treaties.

Finally, one of the essential principles of our common civilization is the peaceful settlement of differences on the basis of established rules and procedures. In this frame of reference, the delegation of certain limited but real powers to a common political authority would appear to be a *necessary* consequence of the very principle of our civilization.

J. ROBERT SCHAETZEL

An Atlantic Partnership

Ambassador J. Robert Schaetzel served as Deputy Assistant Secretary of State for Atlantic Affairs (Department of State) from 1962 until 1966 when he was appointed U. S. Representative to the European Communities in Brussels. He has had a long civil service career (1945–present) in the Department of State where he has served consecutively in the areas of International Trade Policy, Economic Affairs, and Disarmament and Atomic Energy. In 1961 Ambassador Schaetzel was appointed Special Assistant to the Under Secretary of State for Economic Affairs and then Special Assistant to the Under Secretary of State.

THERE ARE BASICALLY THREE broad alternative ways in which European and North American relations can be organized. There is first the national-state system. Its most evident appeal is that everyone is used to it. It is a system that permits people to continue to do what comes naturally. For those in the United States who look with apprehension on a united Europe and anticipate that such a Europe might have a mind of its own, the nineteenth-century arrangement of nation-states has the advantage of offering the known rather than the unknown dangers. With the largest European state (Germany) having a gross national product about 15 percent of that of the United States, there is not much reason for Americans to fear that even the major European states will individually be able to dictate Western policy. In a word, this pattern of Atlantic organization seems to hold the seductive promise of conscious or unconscious American dominance which some see as a kind of American Commonwealth.

The second arrangement is the Atlantic Union or the federated Atlantic Community. In the late 1940s, in the immediate aftermath

Excerpted by special permission from *Foreign Affairs* (April, 1966), Vol. 44, No. 3. Copyright by the Council on Foreign Relations, Inc., New York.

of a world war that changed all things and for a time made all things seem possible, the goal of a federated Atlantic union attracted considerable attention. Congressional resolutions endorsed the principle. Those who have tirelessly advocated this course do so with the highest of motives. They appreciate the common cultural and political heritage of Europe and America and see clearly the need to organize the great potential strength of the North Atlantic. They urge that Washington take the lead in convening an Atlantic convention, drawing on the historic achievement of the Philadelphia Convention of 1787. They are enthusiastic over the prospect of a twentieth-century conference framing a charter for a North Atlantic federation.

Whatever chance there was for Atlantic Union existed during the dark postwar years. Then a destitute and politically demoralized Europe had few choices and in desperation was ready to explore almost any solution. With new-found strength the United States, freed from the foreign policy restraints of the past, showed a remarkable willingness to innovate and, not least important, had been forced by 1948 to the conclusion that the U.S.S.R. under Stalin was bent on pursuing its crusade for world domination. Yet even in this unique period of ferment and creativity, Atlantic Union never became a matter of serious inter-governmental negotiation. Today, while the goal remains credible and the motivations unassailable, it is hard to discern either popular or governmental support for this approach—especially in Europe. Some advocates of Atlantic federation argue that this approach would appeal to the French Government. But if a central issue in the current intra-European dispute has been French resistance to majority rule among six nations and unwillingness to concede powers to a common executive body, by what jump in logic can one assume French willingness to accept similar political restraints in a larger Atlantic Community, one, moreover, inevitably dominated by the United States?

There are problems common to both the system of national states and Atlantic Union. An overriding issue is the great and growing disparity in power—political, military and economic— between the United States and even the strongest of the European nations. While American dominance in both these systems may seem an attractive advantage to some Americans, the disadvantageous side effects should be recognized. The essential difficulty of a grossly disparate trans-Atlantic relationship is that it forces America to assume the major responsibility for the security of the free world.

We have fallen heir to this burden at a time in history when leadership offers none of the real or even the illusory benefits that spurred Europe on in its imperial adventures of the eighteenth and nineteenth centuries. Nor do Americans show any sign of enjoying the isolated splendor of world leadership. Psychologically we are a people who want colleagues and partners.

It is in connection with this point that the disparity of power becomes significant. Given the limited size and capacity of the individual European nations, they are neither willing nor able to play more than suppporting roles. And the United States, carrying a large share of the burdens and the costs, cannot realistically share responsibility for policy decisions with reluctant junior associates. The axiom is inverted and becomes "no representation without taxation." A vicious circle sets in. We want European participation, but cannot fully share decisions in the absence of a European contribution commensurate with our own; the Europeans are neither organized to make this contribution nor much interested in doing so. . . .

The third policy choice is the concept of partnership with a uniting Europe. "Partnership" is a confining word. But as used by President Kennedy in 1962 and subsequently by President Johnson, it conveys a sweeping concept—the idea of a united Europe with which the United States could work in close cooperation and on equal terms.

Such a course of policy would by no means be free of problems or uncertainties. The uncertainties of the moment are all too evident, with the Kennedy Round of tariff negotiations, for instance, effectively stalled due to the unresolved Common Market crisis. Even assuming that agreement is reached among the Europeans and a sense of common purpose restored, the way of the Atlantic partners is bound to be difficult. The sheer magnitude and novelty of the task of unifying Europe will preoccupy the Europeans. Caught up in these affairs, their governments will be less inclined, at least in the short run, to give attention even to what they would agree are common problems, or to give an equal priority to urgent international questions.

A degree of "European nationalism" is also inevitable—not aggressive nationalism but an introspective egocentricity, a primary concern with the development of a united Europe. Nor can we expect that European attitudes will be wholly free of anti-Americanism. Just as giant America is one stimulus toward forming a united Europe, so the evolution of Atlantic relations will be colored by

envy, resentment and, on occasion, policies that self-consciously set
Europe apart from the United States.

However, seen from any distance and in any perspective, the
basic interests of the United States and Europe appear to converge
rather than conflict. We have few, if any, doctrinal differences. Our
complex industrial societies are theoretically and practically interconnected; we struggle with largely identical problems. We may
fall into disagreement on solutions, as Americans or Europeans do
among themselves. It is hard to visualize conflict among the Atlantic
nations arising out of differing ambitions or objectives toward the
less developed world. Outside the minds of propagandists and un-
regenerate Marxists, there is no European or American colonialist
impulse. The problem today is precisely the opposite: how to
restrain the European—and our own—instinct to withdraw, to find
other shoulders to which the security and development burden can
be transferred.

Europeans occasionally see hypocrisy in the American advocacy
of European unity. If the loss of national sovereignty is good for
Europe, why isn't it good for America? One answer is that Americans
today are less aware of a need to consider limits on their freedom
of national action. Willingness to consider restraints will presumably
occur in time of crisis or when Europe is so organized as to make
such changes or restraints attractive, necessary or inevitable. . . .

In even this abbreviated analysis it becomes clear that the choice
is essentially between a system of national European states and
Atlantic partnership. In this context Atlantic union—or federation—
runs as a poor third principally because this alternative has so little
appeal to the Europeans at the present time. It should be noted,
however, that at some point in time interest in Atlantic partnership
and in the goal of Atlantic union may very well converge. There is
nothing in the concept of Atlantic partnership that precludes an
eventual fusing of a united Europe and the United States.

But even if one accepts the validity of Atlantic partnership, it
is a policy that for the moment is stalled. There is no effective
European partner. Americans are acutely conscious of the fact that
the world will not stand still waiting for the Atlantic nations to
sort out their affairs. Since we are an impatient people we approach
foreign policy with much the same attitude that impels us to turn
in two-year-old automobiles. The older a policy, the more suspect
it is. But the most suspect is the old policy that doesn't seem to be
yielding results. This emotional reaction could hardly be at greater

variance with the history of large political or social ideas. All movements that have basically changed men's thoughts or the organization of their affairs have had to overcome deep resistance and
inertia. . . .

But the fact remains that the policy of Atlantic partnership for
the moment is stagnant. What can be done? There should certainly
be a clear sense of "strategic direction." This should be in the
minds of government officials and of the people who must make
their own private decisions. This strategic direction manifests itself in
periodic statements. . . . But there is also the question of how we
and the Europeans deal with immediate problems. For instance, despite the importance and urgency of the Kennedy Round negotiations, we and other participants in the discussions have recognized
that the E.E.C. must straighten out its own affairs before the talks
can be resumed in earnest. At the same time, we have recognized
that the E.E.C. is central to these negotiations and that the Community should be dealt with as a unit.

A second example can be found in the European nuclear problem, whatever its ultimate disposition may be. The United States
has indicated its willingness, in response to European desires, to
envisage a "European clause" in any plan that may eventually
emerge. The purpose of this clause would be to assure that certain
options remained open. Without predicting what would happen in
the organization of Europe, or indeed even indicating an American
preference, the intent of this clause would be to say, "if at some
juncture in the future a united Europe should come into being, able
to make the most fundamental decisions of peace and war, then
whatever we have agreed to now should be subject to review and
renegotiation in the light of these fundamental changes." We should
face the short term, therefore, with two thoughts in mind: to deal
with immediate problems when we can in such a fashion as to advance us toward our strategic goals and, when this is not possible,
at least to avoid foreclosing any options that both we and the
Europeans wish to leave open.

It can be asked whether the sweeping goal of Atlantic partnership is not too ambitious. Today we accept as a matter of course
audacity in the pure sciences, but seem reluctant to match it with
similar audacity in our political behavior. It is generally argued
that great political changes are possible only in times of stress or
acute and evident danger. I take issue with this point of view. But
if political innovation requires danger as a prod, then we have

danger in abundance, even if it appears in ambiguous form. If comprehended, it should produce the stimulus out of which new, creative political ideas should emerge and persevere. One framework within which such ideas should take shape is the embryonic concept of an Atlantic partnership.

I have tried to bring out facts and identify basic interests rather than rely on speculation and hope. Yet the most significant "fact" may well be the tenacious hold the dream of unity has on the European mind. Ideas that lead to profound political change have generally been simple and easily grasped. European union is such an idea. Americans, in all prudence, should weigh this sentiment, recognize that the idea of unity has a firm hold on the minds of Europeans, and note that the new European institutions have worked and begun to meet the challenge of complex industrial societies.

But these conclusions do not help much in predicting the timing or the character of future steps. Not even dedicated Europeans are either optimistic or clear about the short run. A sense of perspective is essential. What the Europeans are about today and tomorrow— and, hopefully, the day after tomorrow in cooperation with the United States—is to penetrate new political frontiers. They are trying to find new methods of coping with the realities of their own political world that will meet the requirements and interests of their people. "Atlantic interdependence" is our way of agreeing that old patterns are inadequate and that we stand ready to consider new relationships. It is inconceivable to me that this nation, with its gift for political thought and record of successful political innovation, will be found wanting in the presence of a united Europe able and prepared to collaborate with us in the tasks that lie ahead.

Suggestions for Further Reading

Although European integration did not emerge as a serious issue for governmental decision-making until the post-war period, the history of the idea of European union is a long one and may provide some interesting insights into "new" problems with older antecedents. A short and concise summary is presented in Sydney D. Bailey's *United Europe—A Short History of the Idea* (National News-Letter—London, 1948). Of special value for the student interested in the common spiritual and cultural heritage of Europe is the volume, *Europe and the Europeans* (Chatto and Windus—London, 1957), a conference report edited by Max Beloff and prepared at the request of the Council of Europe. For a more detailed historical review see Rene Albrecht-Carrié, *One Europe: The Historical Background of European Unity* (Doubleday—New York, 1965).

Among the early 20th Century proponents of European unity, none assumes a more central role in the inter-war period than Count Richard N. Coudenhove-Kalergi who, as author and activist, ". . . carried on, almost singlehandedly, the struggle to enlist the interest and enthusiasm of European statesmen and the general public in his plan to establish what he called the 'United States of Europe'. . ."* Both that struggle and the ideas he propagated are best described in his own works: *Pan-Europe* (Alfred A. Knopf—New York, 1926), *Europe Must Unite* (Plymouth Mayflower Press—London, 1939), *Crusade for Pan-Europe* (G. P. Putnam's Sons—New York, 1943), and *An Idea Conquers the World* (Hutchinson—London, 1953). Another early book of note which advocated European unification is *The United States of Europe* (George G. Harrap & Co. Ltd.—London, 1930) by Edouard Herriot, a former French Premier who, along with Aristide Briand, was a supporter of Coudenhove-Kalergi's Pan-Europe and a French proponent of a United States of Europe.

Among the general works on post-war European integration, Arnold Zurcher's *The Struggle to Unite Europe: 1940–1958* (New

---

* Arnold J. Zurcher, *The Struggle to Unite Europe: 1940–1958* (New York University Press—New York, 1958), p. 3.

York University Press—New York, 1958) provides excellent background for the years included, particularly in depicting the linkage between the European Movement and such organizational accomplishments as the Council of Europe and the European Coal and Steel Community. *The Uniting of Europe* (Stanford University Press —Stanford, 1958) by Ernst Haas deals with the same period, but specifically analyzes the integration process as it occurs at both the national and supranational levels. Along with others, Haas also contributed to papers presented at the Grotius Seminar of 1961 under the title, *Limits and Problems of European Integration* (Nijhoff —The Hague, 1963) and wrote one of the outstanding works on modern international integration, *Beyond the Nation-State: Functionalism and International Organization* (Stanford University Press— Stanford, 1964). Additional volumes dealing with the general question of European unity include: Michael Curtis, *Western European Integration* (Harper and Row—New York, 1965); Michael T. Florinsky, *Integrated Europe?* (Macmillan—New York, 1955); C. Grove Haines, ed., *European Integration* (The Johns Hopkins Press—Baltimore, 1957); Walter Hallstein, *United Europe: Challenge and Opportunity* (Harvard University Press—Cambridge, 1962); U. W. Kitzinger, *The Politics and Economics of European Integration* (Frederick A. Praeger—New York, 1963); Richard Mayne, *The Community of Europe* (W. W. Norton & Co., Inc.—New York, 1962); and Arthur H. Robertson, *European Institutions: Co-operation, Integration, Unification* (Praeger—New York, 1959). Special note should be taken of the Winter 1964 issue of *Daedalus* entitled "A New Europe" and published by the American Academy of Arts and Sciences; in addition to the provocative article by Raymond Aron on "Old Nations, New Europe," it contains several more excellent pieces.

The movement for closer European Union received much of its immediate post-war impetus from the non-governmental organization, the European Movement, and from the leadership of individual European statesmen who supported it. Thus, Winston Churchill, as chairman of the United Europe Movement in Britain, spurred the drive for European cooperation with his numerous speeches both in Britain and on the continent. These were edited by his son, Randolph, and appear in two volumes, *The Sinews of Peace* (Cassell & Co. Ltd.—London, 1948) and *Europe Unite* (Cassell & Co. Ltd.— London, 1950). Churchill's earlier speeches may be found in the three-volume compilation, *The War Speeches of The Rt. Hon. Winston*

S. Churchill (Cassell & Co. Ltd.—London, 1952), edited by Charles Eade. Another useful source in this respect is the European Movement's *European Movement and the Council of Europe* (Hutchinson & Co. Ltd.—London, 1950).

Largely through the efforts of the European Movement, the Council of Europe was created in 1949 as the intergovernmental political institution within which many of the subsequent discussions and decisions regarding further integration took place. In addition to the Council's own records and debates, two of the best expositions of its activities and problems are Arthur H. Robertson, *The Council of Europe: Its Structure, Functions and Achievements* (Frederick A. Praeger—New York, 1961) and Kenneth Lindsay, *Towards a European Parliament* (Council of Europe—Strasbourg, 1958). Lindsay's *European Assemblies: The Experimental Period, 1949-1959* (Frederick A. Praeger—New York, 1960), though broader in scope, is also particularly valuable for its comparison of the various assemblies, among them the Consultative Assembly of the Council of Europe, co-existent in Europe at the same time. For a political analysis of decision-making within the Council as an intergovernmental and non-supranational organization, Ernst Haas' *Consensus Formation in the Council of Europe* (University of California Press—Berkeley, 1960) should not be overlooked.

But European integration did not occur solely, or even primarily, in the political arena. Rather, it was the need for economic recovery and the Marshall Plan's prescription of European cooperation and American aid which led to one of the most successful institutions for cooperation in the post-war period, the Organization for European Economic Cooperation. Though books, especially paperbacks, abound on the Common Market and NATO, there is almost a dearth of material *specifically* related to the Marshall Plan and the OEEC. One notable exception is Harry B. Price, *The Marshall Plan and Its Meaning* (Cornell University Press—Cornell, 1955). David Wightman's *Economic Cooperation in Europe* (Frederick A. Praeger—New York, 1956) provides an excellent source of information and insights on the U.N.'s Economic Commission for Europe, but the thrust of the book does not fall on the OEEC. More to the point is William Diebold, *Trade and Payments in Western Europe: A Study in Economic Cooperation, 1947-1951* (Harper—New York, 1952), but the study concentrates mainly on economic, not political, policies and problems.

An early analysis of the American aid program can be found in

Seymour Harris, *The European Recovery Program* (Harvard University Press—Cambridge, 1948), and somewhat later Brown and Opie produced their thorough and admirable study of *American Foreign Assistance* (The Brookings Institution—Washington, 1953); both books, however, examine European economic cooperation very largely in terms of American interests and policies. The European assessment is expressed well, but briefly, in the OEEC pamphlet, "European Economic Cooperation" (Survey Prepared by the O.E.E.C.—May, 1951), and for the British viewpoint, both on the OEEC and on cooperation in general, the study by the Royal Institute of International Affairs of "Britain in Western Europe" (R.I.I.A.—London, 1956) can not be surpassed. A large section of Max Beloff's *The United States and the Unity of Europe* (The Brookings Institution—Washington, 1963) examines the negotiations surrounding the creation of the OEEC and its implementation both in the United States and in Europe; the book also deals with U.S.—European relations in other areas as well.

It has been pointed out that the military incentives for closer European cooperation paralleled the economic incentives and led to the creation of such collective defense pacts as the Brussels Treaty Organization and NATO; later, with the failure of EDC, Western European Union was formed as an adjunct to the North Atlantic Alliance and, politically, as a device to rearm Germany and integrate her into NATO. The West European BTO, or "Western Union," as it was called, provided many of the precedents which were later incorporated into the trans-Atlantic NATO; a useful study in terms of the former is Andrew and Frances Boyd's *Western Union: A Study of the Trend Toward European Unity* (Public Affairs Press—Washington, 1949), while Sir W. Eric Beckett examines both organizations in relation to the United Nations in *The North Atlantic Treaty, The Brussels Treaty and The Charter of the United Nations* (Stevens & Sons Ltd.—London, 1950). Lord Ismay's book, *NATO: The First Five Years, 1949–1954* (Bosch-Utrecht—Netherlands, 1955), provides a classic portrayal of the structure, activities, and development of NATO up until the mid–50's as seen by an astute diplomat from the inside. More recent general volumes include George E. G. Catlin, *The Atlantic Community* (Coram—London, 1959); Cerny and Briefs, eds., *NATO in Quest of Cohesion* (Frederick A. Praeger—New York, 1965); Cottrell and Dougherty, *The Politics of the Atlantic Alliance* (Frederick A. Praeger—New York, 1964); Löwenstein and Zühlsdorff, *NATO and the Defense of the West* (Frederick A. Praeger—New

York, 1962); Frank Munk, *Atlantic Dilemma* (Oceana—New York, 1964); Timothy W. Stanley, *NATO in Transition: The Future of the Atlantic Alliance* (Frederick A. Praeger—New York, 1965); Robert Strausz—Hupe, *et al., Building the Atlantic World* (Harper and Row—New York, 1963); and Wilcox and Haviland, eds., *The Atlantic Community: Progress and Prospects* (Frederick A. Praeger—New York, 1963).

There are also several specialized works on NATO which specifically refer to some of the issues discussed in this volume. For analyses of the interrelationships between NATO and European Union see both M. Margaret Ball, *NATO and the European Union Movement* (Frederick A. Praeger—New York, 1959) and Ben T. Moore, *NATO and the Future of Europe* (Harper—New York, 1958). Klaus E. Knorr discusses military aspects of the alliance in *NATO and American Security* (Princeton University Press—Princeton, 1959). Strategy and military policy also constitute a large segment of Alastair Buchan's *NATO in the 1960's: The Implications of Interdependence* (Frederick A. Praeger—New York, 1963), although Buchan then proceeds to examine the imperatives of U.S.-European interdependence and argues for the development of common policies. Robert E. Osgood also relates the changing nature of U.S. military strategy to the problems of NATO in his book, *NATO, the Entangling Alliance* (University of Chicago Press—Chicago, 1962) and Raymond Aron surveys the major developments of Western strategic theory and examines current Atlantic problems in *The Great Debate: Theories of Nuclear Strategy* (Doubleday & Co., Inc.—New York, 1965). The specifics of the EDC imbroglio form the substance of *France Defeats EDC* (Frederick A. Praeger—New York, 1957) by Raymond Aron and Daniel Lerner.

The continuing issues of European integration as delineated in this volume not only arise out of the broader context of post-war economic recovery and military cooperation, however, but relate even more directly to the closer integration achieved among "the six" and to their relationships with one another, with the rest of Western Europe, with Eastern Europe, and, across the Atlantic, with the United States. As background to these problems, some of the general studies of European integration mentioned above are most useful, as well as such commentaries on the Common Market as Jean F. Deniau, *The Common Market* (Frederick A. Praeger—New York, 1960); W. O. Henderson, *The Genesis of the Common Market* (Frank Cass—London, 1962); Jensen and Walter, *The Common Market: Economic Integra-*

tion in Europe (J. B. Lippincott Co.—Philadelphia, 1965); U. W. Kitzinger, *The Challenge of the Common Market* (B. Blackwell— Oxford, 1962); Lawrence B. Krause, ed., *The Common Market: Progress and Controversy* (Prentice-Hall—Englewood Cliffs, N.J., 1964); Nystrom and Malof, *The Common Market: European Community in Action* (Van Nostrand—Princeton, N.J., 1962); and Shanks and Lambert, *The Common Market Today—And Tomorrow* (Frederick A. Praeger—New York, 1962). For those students interested in Common Market and NATO relations with the developing areas, see M.W.J.W. Broemeijer, *Developing Countries and NATO* (A. W. Sythoff—Leyden, 1963), Rupert Emerson, "The Atlantic Community and the Emerging Countries" in Wilcox and Haviland, *The Atlantic Community* (Frederick A. Praeger—New York, 1963), and Chapter 7 of Jensen and Walter, *The Common Market: Economic Integration in Europe* (J. B. Lippincott Co.—Philadelphia, 1965).

Additional readings on the specific issues herein included can often be found only as pamphlets or as chapters of broader volumes. The issue of nationalism versus supranationalism, for example, can claim few books devoted purely to itself. A notable exception is the recent volume by Peter Hay, *Federalism and Supranational Organizations* (University of Illinois Press—Urbana, 1966). The degree to which traditional national powers have been delegated to or assumed by "supranational" organs of the European Community can also be assessed by closer examination of the various institutions and organs themselves. Thus, both *Judicial Control of the European Communities* (Stevens—London, 1962) by Gerhard Bebr and *The Court of the European Communities: New Dimension in International Adjudication* (Nijhoff—The Hague, 1964) by Werner Feld examine the legal aspects of the European Community and the novel powers of the European Court. The broader legal implications of the European Community are examined in A. H. Robertson, *The Law of International Institutions in Europe* (Oceana—New York, 1961) and, more recently, in Stuart A. Scheingold, *The Rule of Law in European Integration* (Yale University Press—New Haven, 1965). The development of parliamentary consultation, if not control, is described and analyzed in Murray Forsyth's *The Parliament of the European Communities* (Political and Economic Planning—London, 1964) and it was also effectively done in Kenneth Lindsay, *European Assemblies: The Experimental Period, 1949–1959,* mentioned above. Supranationalism, as it emerged in the earliest of the supranational organizations, the European Coal and Steel Community, is alluded to in some of the major studies of that organization: William Diebold, *The Schuman Plan: A Study in Economic Cooperation, 1950-1959* (Frederick A. Praeger—New York, 1959); Louis Lister, *Europe's Coal and Steel Community—An Experiment in Economic Union* (Twentieth Century Fund—New York, 1960; Henry L. Mason, *The European Coal and Steel Community—Experiment in Supranationalism* (Nijhoff—The Hague, 1955); and Donald G. Valentine, *The Court of Justice of the European Coal and Steel Community* (Nijhoff—The Hague, 1954).

Proponents of a supranational Europe have been more prolific in proselytizing their cause than the non-believers whose sole major spokesman has been General de Gaulle (see below for suggested works). Of the advocates, Jean Monnet and Paul-Henri Spaak are perhaps the most well-known and respected; neither has written major books on the subject, however, and their ideas are perhaps best gleaned from articles or from their several speeches, although J. H. Huizinga's *Mr. Europe: A Political Biography of Paul-Henri Spaak* (Frederick A. Praeger—New York, 1961) does present the general position of M. Spaak. Paul Reynaud, another champion of federal integration, presents his views in *Unite or Perish: A Dynamic Program for a United Europe* (Simon and Schuster—New York, 1951). A more theoretical approach can be found in both Hans Kohn, *Nationalism in the North Atlantic Community* (Research Monograph No. 3, Foreign Policy Research Institute, University of Pennsylvania, 1965) and in Karl W. Deutsch, *Political Community and the North Atlantic Area* (Princeton University Press—Princeton, 1957). Related in focus, though not in terminology, is Arthur W. Macmahon's *Federalism—Mature and Emergent* (Doubleday—New York, 1955).

The relationship of Britain to the continent can best be understood from two perspectives: one, the history of British policies toward Europe and the changing conditions of world power which have affected those policies; two, the interests of the United Kingdom beyond Europe—namely, in the Commonwealth and Empire and in her trans-Atlantic ties with the United States. Both perspectives are eloquently expressed in Sir Oliver Frank's little volume of Reith lectures entitled, *Britain and the Tide of World Affairs* (Oxford University Press—London, 1955). James Joll also provides necessary historical background in his edited book of speeches and writings on *Britain and Europe* (Nicholas Kaye Ltd.—London, 1950). A more contemporary analysis which relates past attitudes to present realities is the excellent booklet by a Royal Institute of International Affairs study group, *Britain in Western Europe* (R.I.I.A.—London, 1956).

Perhaps the best general survey, however, which is specifically directed to British policies toward European integration is Miriam Camps' *Britain and the European Community, 1955-1963* (Princeton University Press—Princeton, 1964); it not only relates the traditional views which guided British policies toward the continent, but why and how they changed, and how the ultimate decision to join was finally made—and rebuffed. An interesting examination of the French veto itself may be found in Nora Beloff, *The General Says No: Britain's Exclusion from Europe* (Penguin Books—London, 1963). Other works dealing with Britain and European Union include Economic Intelligence Unit, *Britain and Europe* (Economic Intelligence Unit—London, 1957); Hans J. Heiser, *British Policy with Regard to the Unification Efforts of the European Continent* (A. W. Sythoff—Leyden, 1959); U. W. Kitzinger, *Britain, Europe and Beyond: Essays in European Politics* (Leyden, 1964); Drew Middleton, *The Supreme Choice: Britain and Europe* (Knopf—New York, 1963); John Pinder, *Britain and the Common Market* (Cresset—London, 1961); Shanks and Lambert, Parts I and III of *The Common Market Today—And Tomorrow* (Frederick A. Praeger—New York, 1962); and E. Strauss, *European Reckoning: The Six and Britain's Future* (Allen and Unwin—London, 1962). Tied to the British position is the whole question of EFTA—the European Free Trade Association or "Outer Seven"—and its relationship to the Common Market. Two recommended books in this area are Emile Benoit's *Europe at Sixes and Sevens: The Common Market, The Free Trade Association, and the United States* (Columbia University Press—New York, 1961) and Frederick V. Meyer's *The European Free Trade Association: An Analysis of the "Outer Seven"* (Frederick A. Praeger—New York, 1960).

The German problem in regard to West European integration cannot be isolated from the broader problem of German reunification. For background on the division of Germany, the position of Berlin, and German policies in world politics, see McInnis, Hiscocks, and Spencer, *The Shaping of Postwar Germany* (Frederick A. Praeger —New York, 1960). Another general exposition on the division of Germany and the potential problems it evokes is presented in Gerald Freund, *Germany Between Two Worlds* (Harcourt-Brace—New York, 1961); a short economic analysis may be found in the booklet, *Germany Between East and West* (National Planning Association— Washington, D.C., 1960), by Wolfgang F. Stolper. F. Roy Willis' *France, Germany, and the New Europe, 1945-1963* (Stanford University

Press—Stanford, 1965) provides an historical review of Franco-German politics in the context of postwar European integration. For specific reference to the Common Market, see E. Strauss, *Common Sense About the Common Market: Germany and Britain in Post-War Europe* (Allen and Unwin—London, 1958). For a German point of view, see the volume by Heinrich von Brentano, *Germany and Europe: Reflections on German Foreign Policy* (Frederick A. Praeger—New York, 1964). Frederick H. Hartmann's *Germany Between East and West: The Reunification Problem* (Prentice-Hall, Inc.—Englewood Cliffs, N. J., 1965), from which the selection in this volume is excerpted, provides a sound and concise analysis of the reunification problem.

The division between East and West, however, though epitomized in the German case, obviously extends beyond Germany to the whole of Europe and further complicates the already complex problem of West European unification. An excellent collection of essays on this topic may be found in Collier and Glaser, eds., *Western Integration and the Future of Eastern Europe* (Regnery—Chicago, 1964). For a fairly recent analysis of East-West trade, see John P. De Gara, *Trade Relations between the Common Market and the Eastern Bloc* (College of Europe—Bruges, 1964). Though East European views on Western integration are difficult to find, short articles on the subject sometimes appear in *Eastern Europe,* ideological discussions in *Kommunist,* and more academic analyses in *World Marxist Review.* The student will also be well rewarded for a serious perusal of the various speeches of General de Gaulle on the overall topic of East-West relations and, specifically, of those elaborating upon his concept of "Europe to the Urals." Some of them may be found in *Major Addresses, Statements and Press Conferences of General Charles de Gaulle* (May 19, 1958—January 31, 1964) published by the Press and Information Division of the French Embassy, New York.

United States—West European relations are inextricably bound to the political and military problems of NATO, but for purposes of the issue-orientation of this volume, an attempt has been made to separate, as far as possible, those works concentrating on NATO as such (cited above), and those more specifically concerned with American relations with the European Community. Among the latter, the July, 1963 issue of *The Annals* (Volume 348) of The American Academy of Political and Social Science is devoted entirely to the topic of *The New Europe: Implications for the United States;*

the selections in this volume, edited by James C. Charlesworth, are both pertinent and interesting. F. S. C. Northrop's *European Union and United States Foreign Policy* (Macmillan—New York, 1954) and Max Beloff's *The United States and the Unity of Europe* (The Brookings Institution—Washington, 1963) provide general introductions to the topic, while Robert Kleiman in *Atlantic Crisis: American Diplomacy Confronts a Resurgent Europe* (Norton—New York, 1964), George Lichtheim in *Europe and America: The Future of the Atlantic Community* (Thomas and Hudson—London, 1963), and Ronald Steel in *The End of Alliance: America and the Future of Europe* (Viking—New York, 1964) deal with the developing strains in U.S.—European relationships and the implications of those problems for future policies. Economic relations are discussed both in Randall Hinshaw's *The European Community and American Trade* (Frederick A. Praeger—New York, 1964) and in Don D. Humphrey's *The United States and the Common Market* (Frederick A. Praeger—New York, 1962).

The more specific questions regarding Europe's role *vis-a-vis* the United States assume two major aspects: one, whether Europe should pursue policies independently of the United States or within the agreed limits of an Atlantic framework, and two, if within an Atlantic framework, whether the relationship should be one of partnership or closer union. United States Government documents of special interest in this regard include the U.S. Senate Staff Study on *Problems and Trends in Atlantic Partnership I–II: Some Comments on the European Economic Community and NATO* (Sen. Docs. No. 132 and 21—1962 and 1963); *The Atlantic Alliance: Allied Comment,* a committee print prepared by the Subcommittee on National Security and International Operations for the use of the Committee on Government Operations; and both the Hearings and Reports of the Subcommittee on Europe of the House Committee on Foreign Affairs concerning *The Crisis in NATO* (89th Congress, 2nd Session —1966). David P. Calleo, *Europe's Future: The Grand Alternatives* (Horizon Press—New York, 1965), Roy Pryce, *The Political Future of the European Community* (John Marshbank—London, 1962) and Max Kohnstamm, *The European Community and Its Role in the World* (University of Missouri Press, 1965) provide general analyses on the future of the European Community. Works devoted more directly to the "partnership—community" issue include: Kurt Birrenbach, *The Future of the Atlantic Community: Toward European-American Partnership* (Frederick A. Praeger—New York, 1963); Mority J. Bonn, *Whither Europe—Union or Partnership?* (Cohen and West—London, 1952); Livingston Hartley, *Atlantic Challenge* (Oceana—New York, 1965); Christian A. Herter, *Toward an Atlantic Community* (Harper and Row—New York, 1963); Henry A. Kissinger, *The Troubled Partnership* (McGraw-Hill—New York, 1965); Joseph Kraft, *The Grand Design: From Common Market to Atlantic Partnership* (Harper and Row—New York, 1962); Massimo Salvadori, *NATO, a Twentieth-Century Community of Nations* (Van Nostrand—Princeton, N.J., 1957); Clarence Streit, *Freedom's Frontier: Atlantic Union Now* (Harper and Row—New York, 1961); and Pierre Uri, *Partnership for Progress* (Harper and Row—New York, 1963). The primary political dissident of an integrated Atlantic partnership or community and a strong advocate of an "independent" Europe is, of course, Charles de Gaulle. In addition to the citations already mentioned, for his views on this issue see two recent books on de Gaulle, Robert Aron's *An Explanation of De Gaulle* (Harper and Row—New York, 1965) and Roy C. Macridis' *De Gaulle: Implacable Ally* (Harper and Row—New York, 1966).

Final bibliographical mention should be made of those works dealing with the theory and processes of integration. Because of the number of these volumes, however, a simple listing may suffice: Bela Balassa, *The Theory of Economic Integration* (Richard D. Irwin, Inc., Homewood, Illinois, 1961); Karl W. Deutsch, *et al., The Integration of Political Communities* (J. B. Lippincott—Philadelphia, 1964); Amatai Etzioni, *Political Unification: A Comparative Analysis of Leaders and Forces* (Holt, Rinehart, and Winston—New York, 1965); Leon N. Lindberg, *The Political Dynamics of European Economic Integration* (Stanford University Press—Stanford, 1963); George Liska, *Europe Ascendent: The International Politics of Unification* (The Johns Hopkins University Press—Baltimore, 1964); James E. Meade, ed., *Case Studies in European Economic Union: The Mechanics of Integration* (Oxford University Press—Oxford, 1962); Elmer Plischke, ed., *Systems of Integrating the International Community* (Van Nostrand—Princeton, N.J., 1963); Tibor Scitovsky, *Economic Theory and Western European Integration* (Stanford University Press—Stanford, 1958); and Stannwald and Stohler, *Economic Integration: Theoretical Assumptions and Consequences of European Integration* (Princeton University Press—Princeton, 1959).

Some of the most pertinent periodicals on the European Community are the monthly *European Community* (Information Service—Washington Office), the weekly *Common Market News* (Comtel Reuter), and the *Journal of Common Market Studies* (Basil Blackwood, Oxford). For special reference to Britain and Europe, see the *Britain in Europe Review* (published quarterly by Britain in Europe, 43 Parliament Street, London SWI) and the *European Review* which is published every two months (Editorial Offices: 61 Gloucester Place, London W I). The *European Yearbook*, published by the Council of Europe, provides an excellent annual account of the activities of all of the West European organizations, including the three Communities (Nijhoff—The Hague). For the wider issues of Europe and the Atlantic Community, the best periodical sources are *The Atlantic Community Quarterly,* published quarterly by the Atlantic Council of the United States, Washington, and the quarterly *European Atlantic Review* (Manhattan Publishing Co.—New York).